Installing Debian GNU/Linux

Thomas Down

SΛMS

A Division of Macmillan USA
201 West 103rd Street, Indianapolis, Indiana 46290

Installing Debian GNU/Linux

International Standard Book Number: 0-672-31745-1

Library of Congress Catalog Card Number: 99-63617

Printed in the United States of America

First Printing: December, 1999

01   00   99   4   3   2   1

Trademarks

All terms mentioned in this book that are known to be trademarks or service marks have been appropriately capitalized. Sams Publishing cannot attest to the accuracy of this information. Use of a term in this book should not be regarded as affecting the validity of any trademark or service mark.

Warning and Disclaimer

Every effort has been made to make this book as complete and as accurate as possible, but no warranty or fitness is implied. The information provided is on an "as is" basis. The author and the publisher shall have neither liability nor responsibility to any person or entity with respect to any loss or damages arising from the information contained in this book or from the use of the CD or programs accompanying it.

ASSOCIATE PUBLISHER
Angela Wethington

ACQUISITIONS EDITOR
Neil Rowe

DEVELOPMENT EDITOR
Tony Amico

MANAGING EDITOR
Lisa Wilson

PROJECT EDITOR
Dawn Pearson

COPY EDITOR
Kezia Endsley

INDEXER
Christine Nelsen

PROOFREADER
Katherin Bidwell

TECHNICAL EDITOR
Dan Scherf

TEAM COORDINATOR
Karen Opal

MEDIA DEVELOPER
Dave Carson

INTERIOR DESIGNER
Karen Ruggles

COVER DESIGNER
Aren Howell

COPY WRITER
Eric Borgert

PRODUCTION
Dan Harris
Louis Porter Jr.

Contents at a Glance

Table of Contents

About the Author

Thomas Down was born in 1977 and has worked on and off as a freelance programmer and computing journalist. While obtaining a degree in biochemistry, he stumbled upon Linux and has been a dedicated user ever since. He now lives in Cambridge, England and works on techniques for automated genetic analysis. "Installing Debian GNU/Linux" is his first book.

Dedication

To my parents, for listening to all that gobbledygook.

Acknowledgments

This book would not have been possible without the collective effort of tens of thousands of developers, working on the Linux kernel, the associated tools, and the distribution itself. Thank you everyone.

Tell Us What You Think!

As the reader of this book, *you* are our most important critic and commentator. We value your opinion and want to know what we're doing right, what we could do better, what areas you'd like to see us publish in, and any other words of wisdom you're willing to pass our way.

As a Publisher for Sams, I welcome your comments. You can fax, email, or write me directly to let me know what you did or didn't like about this book—as well as what we can do to make our books stronger.

Please note that I cannot help you with technical problems related to the topic of this book, and that due to the high volume of mail I receive, I might not be able to reply to every message.

When you write, please be sure to include this book's title and author as well as your name and phone or fax number. I will carefully review your comments and share them with the author and editors who worked on the book.

Fax: 317-581-4770
Email: opsys@mcp.com
Mail: Angela Wethington
    Sams
    201 West 103rd Street
    Indianapolis, Indiana 46290

CHAPTER 1

Introducing Debian

Linux has been arguably the biggest computing success story of the late '90s. In the space of a few years, an operating system once regarded as the exclusive preserve of a few enthusiasts has gained much respect, and widespread deployment. It is most commonly regarded as an operating system for server applications—especially for running Web sites and other Internet-based services. However, when a Linux system is configured with a modern desktop environment such as Gnome (see Figure 1.1) or KDE, the *user-hostile* image of Linux (and other UNIX-like systems) is not at all deserved. With the help of the desktop environments and a selection of productivity tools, Linux is starting to catch on as a complete desktop computing solution.

What is not always made clear is that Linux is a kernel: just one component—albeit a central one—of a useful operating system. Fortunately, there is no need to build a system from scratch. Many groups and companies offer the Linux kernel plus a comprehensive selection of other software, all packaged and ready to install. Debian GNU/Linux is one of the most established of these distributions.

Why Use Debian?

The availability of multiple distributions is a key aspect of the Linux phenomenon—and competition between the distributions has certainly been important in the evolution of the Linux systems in use today. But the choice is often confusing to the newcomer. What makes Debian the best choice?

For many people, the key issue is its openness. The Linux kernel, and many of the tools used with it, have benefited from development in an open manner. Why should these distributions be assembled by small groups working behind closed doors? Debian development is led by a group of volunteers spread across the Internet, and everyone has the option to join in.

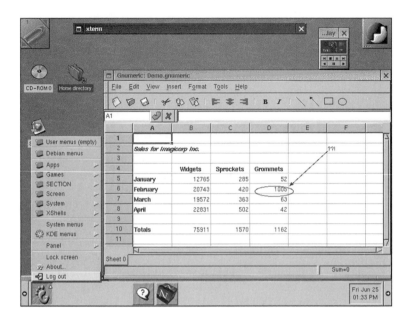

Figure 1.1

Packages such as Gnome add a friendly face, and familiar productivity tools, to the modern UNIX system.

To coordinate work between several hundred active developers (and many more minor contributors and testers) around the world, the Debian project has a well-defined release cycle. Each new version of the system goes through the following states:

Unstable: This refers to the version under development. Modifications can be submitted by anyone. But unlike a closed doors distribution, the latest unstable packages are always widely available, and any user can install either the complete distribution or a single component. The unstable distributions are normally referred to by a code name rather than by a number.

Frozen: Periodically, the current unstable version is frozen. At this point, addition of new features is generally not allowed, and developers concentrate on fixing any bugs.

Stable: After a period of testing and bug-fixing, the frozen distribution is finally allocated a version number and marked as *stable*. This can be considered the *release* version of Debian—CD-ROMs of the distribution are normally based on the stable version.

In addition to its openness, there are good technical reasons for choosing Debian. This open development model has produced a very dependable Linux distribution. Each new version has already undergone a lot of serious public testing before it is released as *stable*. In fact, experience shows that even when a version is described as *unstable*, the term is only relative.

Debian also has a good record for security. It is an unfortunate fact of life that any sophisticated network-capable operating system (such as Linux or Windows NT) is susceptible to various forms of attack. Vulnerabilities can be the result either of user misconfiguration or bugs in security-critical programs. Debian helps to avoid both kinds of vulnerabilities by providing configuration systems that make it easier to secure your system, and by immediately and publicly announcing any security-related problems. The home page of the Debian Web site always carries a list of the latest security alerts, normally with links to simple fixes. Throughout this book, there are tips to help ensure that your computer is set up in a secure manner.

A final difference between distributions, and one that's immediately obvious when installing or upgrading a Linux system, is the system used to package all the different parts of the distributions. The complete Debian distribution consists of several *thousand* packages, ranging from essential utilities to esoteric mathematical applications. No installation will include all of them. Moreover, some depend on other packages, while a few are mutually exclusive.

Package management software allows you to ensure that when you install a package, all of its dependencies will be met. Similarly, if you decide to remove a package, the package manager ensures that all its files are deleted—and you'll be warned first if you're going to break the dependencies of some other package. Debian packages—either those that make up parts of the main distribution or those supplied elsewhere—have filenames ending with the extension .deb. The basic Debian package manager is called dpkg, but in general it is easier to install and remove programs using a frontend called dselect, illustrated in Figure 1.2 and described in detail in Chapter 4, "A Basic Installation."

The Debian package management system is especially helpful when you want to upgrade your system. It can automatically replace all your currently installed packages with newer versions, either from a CD-ROM or downloaded over the Internet. The dselect program makes keeping a Debian installation up-to-date almost painless.

One criticism is sometimes leveled against Debian: Although well-respected, it is currently not the most commonly used distribution. There has been some concern about software being supplied in the RPM package format, developed for the Red Hat Linux distribution (and since adopted by several others). In practice, it is easy to install RPMs on a Debian system, either directly or using the alien tool, which converts them into standard .deb files.

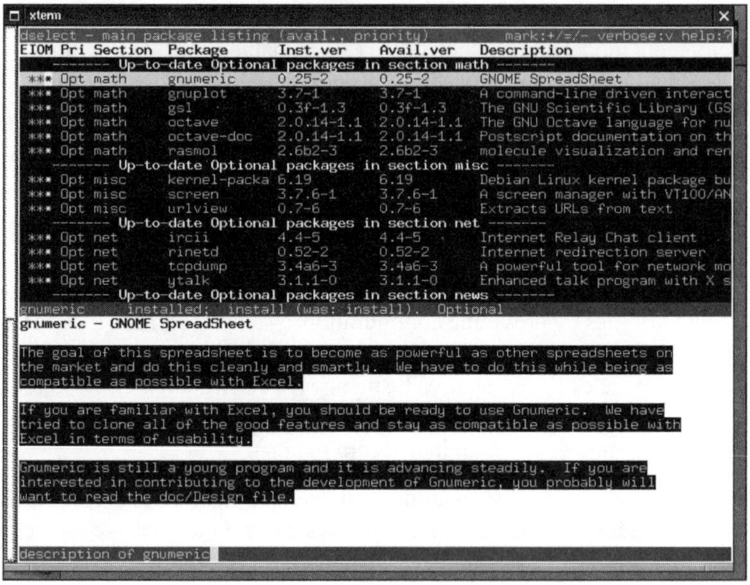

Figure 1.2

The dselect tool allows easy browsing, installation, and upgrading of packages.

Although there are some differences between the structure, contents, and configuration mechanisms of the various Linux distributions, any well-written software should work correctly on all of them. And although some people complain that the availability of competing distributions adds an extra layer of complication to Linux, it is this competition that forces *all* of the distributions to stay up-to-date.

The Main Competition

It would be almost impossible to include a comprehensive list of Linux distributions. Many minor distributions, popular with a small group of users, exist. There are also some cut-down distributions created for specific purposes, such as dedicated Linux-based network routers. The following list simply includes a few major distributions that may be considered reasonable alternatives to Debian.

- **Red Hat:** This is widely considered to be the most commonly used Linux distribution. It is the most open of the major commercial distributions, and all components—including Red Hat's own install and configuration tools—are freely distributable. Nevertheless, the core development still occurs behind closed doors. This is arguably reflected by the number of updates, some security-critical, that tend to appear after each release. Red Hat includes a wide selection of free software, although not as large as Debian's.
- **Caldera OpenLinux:** This is a strongly business-oriented distribution. The installation process seems to be designed with a view to being a drop-in replacement for Windows. Caldera produces what is probably the most

graphical distribution, and it is easy to configure in simple situations. On the other hand, in more complicated cases the graphical tools can prove a hindrance. And, while Caldera uses the RPM package format, there have been some reports of problems running software built for other distributions. Although it is based on free software, the proprietary components mean that Caldera's distribution cannot be redistributed as a whole.

- **Slackware:** This is the oldest distribution still having widespread community support. Unlike the others described here, it isn't based around a special package file format. It also provides significantly less in the way of configuration tools—Slackware users like to set things up themselves.
- **SuSE:** This is another distribution that includes bundled commercial software. This distribution has a strong following in Europe. There is a free demo version, but you have to pay for the complete package with all the bundled software.
- **LinuxPPC:** This is one of a number of distributions which are strongly based on Red Hat. As the name suggests, the main feature is support for PowerPC-based computers, such as recent Apple models.

A Little Debian/Linux History

To understand the philosophy of Debian GNU/Linux—and especially the reasoning behind its name—it is necessary to look at the early history of Linux-based operating systems.

Linux takes its inspiration from the UNIX operating systems, which were originally developed on minicomputers in the 1970s. In the 1980s, UNIX spread to workstation-class computers built by companies such as HP and Sun, and played a major role in the development of the fledgling Internet. During this period, UNIX was normally only supplied with expensive proprietary hardware. In the mean time, commodity PC-type machines were getting more and more powerful. But these usually only ran DOS or early versions of Windows—popular in the home and office markets, but lacking much of the flexibility of UNIX. A few commercial UNIX implementations had been released, but these were expensive, and targeted at fairly restricted markets.

Everything began to change in 1991 when the Finnish student Linus Torvalds decided that he would like to have access to the power of UNIX while using commodity hardware. He started out by developing a small UNIX-like kernel, loosely based on the academic demonstration kernel, Minix. The kernel is the *master program* that controls access to hardware devices, manages the allocation of memory, and provides the scheduling system, while allowing more than one program to run at the same time. In short, Linus was developing the core of a new operating system.

The story could have ended there. But Torvalds chose to release the source code for his kernel, using the name Linux. About this time, Internet access was starting to become more and more common, and many programmers from around the world found the Linux code. While kernels are often not the most obvious part of a modern operating system, they are still fascinating to many programmers, so many of the people who downloaded Linux started experimenting with it. Since they had the complete source code rather than just an executable file, they were able to fix bugs or add new features. These modifications (called *patches*) found their way back to Linus, who included the best of them in the next version.

By the time Linux reached version 2.0 in mid-1996, it had become a powerful and stable kernel which could begin to compete on serious terms with the commercial UNIXes. Moreover, it was free to use, and the availability of source code meant that bugs were fixed very quickly. When an error (widely called the F00F bug) was discovered in Intel's Pentium series of processors—it could crash any Pentium computer simply by sending it a certain sequence of data—it was only a matter of hours before a patch was released that allowed the Linux kernel to recover gracefully when the processor glitched.

Linux development continues today as fast as ever, although the changes aren't always immediately visible. Effort is now concentrated largely on supporting more hardware devices and on boosting the kernel's performance on powerful multiprocessor machines. And while Intel-based PC hardware is still the most popular platform, Linux's design is quite portable, and it will now run on most modern computers, including PowerMacs and Alpha-based workstations.

But while the kernel is an absolutely vital part of any computer operating system, it is not the only piece of software needed to make a machine useful—or even the biggest. For Linux to run at all, the developers needed a *compiler*: the program that translates source code into executable files. They also needed many smaller utility programs to make the system usable: on a UNIX system even the ls command to list files on a disk is a separate program.

Fortunately, when Linux development began, free implementations of most of the key tools were already available. They had been developed as part of the Free Software Foundation's GNU project, set up in the mid-1980s with the stated aim of producing an entire free UNIX-like operating system. By the time Linux development was underway, the GNU suite included most of the vital tools for a workable basic UNIX system—except for the kernel. And it was these tools that made early Linux systems usable. You may like to read more about the FSF's aims, and the reasoning behind the GNU project, on its Web site at http://www.fsf.org/.

As soon as people began to use Linux for anything more than the simplest experimentation, demand began to grow for pre-packaged systems that combine Linux with enough tools to make a usable setup out of the box. The original Linux distributions just consisted of a few floppy disks of essential utilities, with little or nothing in the way of tools to assist in installation and configuration. More gradually, these have been superseded by newer distributions, such as Debian, which add many more application programs, plus increasingly sophisticated tools to make configuring and managing the system easier.

Today a typical Linux distribution includes a vast array of software from the ls command right up to gimp, a sophisticated image editor. Not all the applications included are derived from the GNU project's work. (For instance, the X Window system, which provides the basic services for all windowed software on UNIX, was developed elsewhere.) But without high-quality GNU tools—especially the compiler suite—early Linux systems would certainly have struggled to get off the ground. And GNU tools still make up some of the most important components of any distribution. In recognition of this, Debian has chosen to call its distribution GNU/Linux, signifying that it is based on the GNU system, but with the Linux kernel.

As an aside, the GNU project *did* go on to develop their own kernel, using a rather different internal architecture from Linux. (Although from a user's point of view, the end result will still be a generally UNIX-like system, and run all the same software.) Development of the GNU kernel (called HURD) has been much slower, and it is not yet in general use. However, recently a version of the *unstable* Debian system that uses the HURD kernel has been produced. If HURD does succeed in gathering momentum, future Debian users will have a choice of kernels.

A WORD ABOUT VERSION NUMBERS

Since the Linux kernel is only one part of the complete Debian system, the version numbers of the two do not necessarily match. Indeed, if they do, it is purely coincidental. Debian and the kernel use different version-numbering schemes.

Debian version numbers have the form *major.minor*. A new version number is assigned to each development cycle when it reaches the stable stage. At the time of writing, the current Debian version is 2.1, with the next version—rather curiously code named potato—in the unstable stage.

Linux versioning is a little more complex, with numbers in the form *major.minor.patchlevel*. Like the Debian distribution, stable and unstable versions of Linux exist in parallel. However, unstable Linux kernels are also allocated version numbers, identified by an odd minor version number. So at the time of writing, the current stable kernel is 2.2.10, while new features are being added to development kernels in the 2.3 series. Because bugs in the kernel can have serious consequences, unstable kernels are recommended for active developers or for expert users who need some feature only available in the development series. Note that Debian distributions—even the unstable versions—don't use development kernels.

Licensed to Be Free

The Linux kernel and much of the common software used on Linux systems are free. But this doesn't just mean you don't have to pay for it—according to the definitions used by the Free Software Foundation and the Linux community—true freedom means that you can obtain the source code for a program, modify it, and redistribute it. A commonly used (some would say overused) analogy is that free software is an issue more akin to free speech than free beer.

Many people ask, "Why write free software?" For many developers, the answer is simply because they want to. The Linux kernel started out as a personal project, and even today most of the developers are people with a strong personal interest in the inner workings of operating systems. In other cases, a program sometimes *has* to be written, perhaps for in-house use by company. The question then becomes, "Why *not* release it publicly?" Often, there is nothing to lose, and the original developers can benefit from the input of outside testers and programmers. Obviously, not all GNU/Linux users are themselves programmers; if you ever *do* find yourself developing any software, you should ask yourself whether there is anything to lose by releasing it freely.

Arguably the most free software is placed in the public domain. This software has no license attached to it, and anyone can do exactly what they want with it—including embedding it into a commercial product without giving any credit to the original authors. Such software is rather rare.

The majority of free software is copyrighted and distributed with a license that, while permitting free redistribution, places some mild restrictions to ensure that the authors get the credit. The two most common licenses applied to programs in a Linux distribution are summarized as follows:

- **The General Public License (GPL):** This is the license originally drawn up by the Free Software Foundation to cover the components of the GNU system. It has since been adopted by many programs not written by the FSF—including the Linux kernel. The most significant feature of this license is that, if you give or sell someone a binary copy of a GPLed program, you *must* supply a copy of the source code on request. This license has been drawn up so that it is not possible to produce a proprietary (*non-free*) derivative of a GPLed program.
- **The BSD License:** This is the license applied to software written by programmers at the University of California at Berkeley, and has also been adopted by many other programmers. It is less restrictive than the GPL in that it allows proprietary derivatives of the code. However, it does include a clause requiring that the original developers be acknowledged in any advertising material—a restriction that some people have considered excessive. Confusingly, some programs are distributed under a modified BSD license without this restriction.

From an end user's perspective, the differences between the licenses are usually not particularly important—they all allow you to make unlimited personal and commercial use of the software, and to give a copy to your friends. The biggest differences are apparent when distributing modified versions.

TERMS OF FREEDOM

There have been some arguments about exactly what it takes to make a piece of software free. The increasing number of different software licenses only makes the problem worse. To deal with this question, Debian developers drew up a list of conditions for software freedom: *The Debian Free Software Guidelines.* These comprise a core part of the Debian policy manual, which is available in various formats as a Debian package, and also found on the Debian project Web site. All the core packages of the Debian system have license terms that comply with these guidelines. A few packages that don't comply *are* included, but they are always labeled as non-free. Needless to say, both the GPL and the BSD licenses meet the following guidelines.

1. *Free redistribution*
    The license of a Debian component may not restrict any party from selling or giving away the software as a component of an aggregate software distribution containing programs from several different sources. The license may not require a royalty or other fee for such sale.

2. *Source code*
    The program must include source code, and must allow distribution in source code as well as compiled form.

3. *Derived works*
    The license must allow modifications and derived works, and must allow them to be distributed under the same terms as the license of the original software.

4. *Integrity of the author's source code*
    The license may restrict source code from being distributed in modified form *only* if the license allows the distribution of *patch files* with the source code for the purpose of modifying the program at build time. The license must explicitly permit distribution of software built from modified source code. The license may require derived works to carry a different name or version number from the original software. (This is a compromise. The Debian group encourages all authors not to restrict any files, source or binary, from being modified.)

5. *No discrimination against persons or groups*
    The license must not discriminate against any person or group of persons.

6. *No discrimination against fields of endeavor*
    The license must not restrict anyone from making use of the program in a specific field of endeavor. For example, it may not restrict the program from being used in a business, or from being used for genetic research.

7. *Distribution of license*
    The rights attached to the program must apply to all to whom the program is redistributed without the need for execution of an additional license by those parties.

8. *License must not be specific to Debian*
    The rights attached to the program must not depend on the program's being part of a Debian system. If the program is extracted from Debian and used or distributed without Debian but otherwise within the terms of the program's license, all parties to whom the program is redistributed should have the same rights as those that are granted in conjunction with the Debian system.

9. *License must not contaminate other software*
   The license must not place restrictions on other software that is distributed along with the licensed software. For example, the license must not insist that all other programs distributed on the same medium be free software.

All the core packages of Debian GNU/Linux are distributed under licenses meeting the Debian Free Software Guidelines. But a few packages that don't meet these requirements are included in the non-free section. These are normally free for personal use, but it is your responsibility to check the exact terms of the license. (For instance, the MySQL database system must be licensed if you are to deploy it commercially.)

Debian Today

Debian today is a mature—although, of course, still evolving—distribution. It is suited to a range of applications, from desktop use to running a large corporate Web server. Unlike some of the commercial distributions, every component is freely distributable. A CD-ROM carrying the core of Debian 2.1 is included with this book.

For those with fast Internet connections, it is also possible to download Debian from one of the many officially endorsed mirror sites worldwide. You can find your nearest mirror from the Debian home page at http://www.debian.org/.

Even if you don't want to download the complete distribution, it is often useful to be able to update a few packages in this manner. Setting up the dselect tool to automatically fetch packages over the network when required is explained in Chapter 5, "Making Your Selection."

Debian development remains as active as ever. Future developments are discussed on various Internet mailing lists. Once you have installed Debian and become familiar with its structure and use, you may want to read some of these mailing lists, look at what's going on behind the scenes, and perhaps even join in yourself. There is more information about the Debian mailing lists, and tips for making helpful contributions, in Chapter 11, "And Finally—Welcome to the Community."

Summary

This chapter gives an insight into the history and development of the Debian GNU/Linux distribution. The watchwords are freedom and openness: Anyone who is interested can join in with development work. We return to this theme in the final chapter of this book.

The next two chapters concentrate on the practicalities of preparing for a Debian installation. Chapter 2, "Getting Ready—Hardware," will help you to check that your computer is ready to run a Linux-based operating system. Chapter 3, "Getting Ready—Disk Space," covers the distribution's space requirements, and lists the options available if you need to repartition your disk drive.

CHAPTER 2

Getting Ready—Hardware

The Linux kernel was originally designed to run on PC-type computers based on the Intel i386 (or later) processors. This is still by far the most popular architecture—and the one on which this book concentrates, although most of the information is relevant to other architectures too.

These machines can all trace their ancestry back to the original IBM PC. But since then, a huge number of third parties have produced *clone* PCs. Today it is possible to buy a wide selection of branded PCs. But it is also easy to find *white box* machines, assembled by small local retailers, or even to build your own machine from off-the-shelf components.

The PC explosion has been something of a mixed blessing. Certainly, without the fierce competition between manufacturers, it is unlikely that we would be able to buy high performance computers so cheaply. But in most cases, the industry has been following only *de facto* standards—and even these have sometimes been treated quite flexibly. This diversity can be something of a headache for operating system developers who find they need to support a huge range of hardware.

The good news is that the Linux kernel supports a remarkably high proportion of basic PC hardware—even some evolutionary dead-ends such as the Microchannel architecture used in IBM's PS/2 machines. The kernel should boot on almost any machine made in the last five years.

If you have a standard PC-type machine produced in the last few years, and no specific add-on hardware, you may want to skip the rest of this chapter now and start installing Debian straight away. You can refer back to this chapter if you're having difficulty getting a piece of hardware working under Linux, or if you are thinking about buying new devices for use with your Debian system.

The Base System

The Linux kernel, and many of the basic tools that run on top of it, are relatively undemanding in hardware terms. This isn't to say that they can't take advantage of top of the line hardware—if you're running several big graphical applications, you'll certainly appreciate a fast processor and plenty of memory. But conversely, if you can live without a windowed desktop environment, it's possible to use old hardware as a low-spec server (by sharing a few files and a printer in the home or a small office, for instance) or as a client machine on a network.

Old machines are also useful when you want to try out Linux without touching your current system. Intel i486-based machines, or even early Pentium systems, can often be obtained very cheaply secondhand. While you shouldn't expect too much from such a machine, it will provide an excellent opportunity to experiment with Linux and all its associated tools—especially if you want to learn to get the most from the powerful UNIX command-line interface.

At the other end of the spectrum, many high-end machines—especially those sold for the server market—are now supplied with two or more processors. Support for multiprocessor motherboards was added in kernel 2.0, but has been greatly improved in the new 2.2 series. Debian 2.1 users will probably need to recompile their kernel (see Appendix A, "Kernel Management")—and you may simply wish to upgrade to the latest kernel version.

As of the Linux 2.2 kernel included with the *potato* release of Debian, multiprocessor support will normally be switched on by default, and the system should automatically detect and take advantage of all your processors. Note, however, that the kernel packages are considered to be too critical to be replaced automatically when you upgrade an existing Debian installation: See Appendix A for information about kernel upgrades. You can check that the kernel is correctly detecting all your processors using the command cat /proc/cpuinfo.

There are also a number of manufacturers that make clones of the Intel Pentium series of processors. These work fine under Linux, and can offer better performance for a given price, especially for low-end systems. As a rule of thumb, clone processors from manufacturers such as AMD and Cyrix tend to approximately match the corresponding Intel devices for performance when running *integer* instructions (simple operations where the mathematical engine of the processor is working only with whole numbers). But they can suffer when executing the more complex floating point instructions. Traditionally, the users who are most likely to notice floating point performance are those who work with complex scientific application, and players of games which use 3D graphics. Clone processors are generally not suitable for use in multiprocessor systems.

The exception to this is the Athlon processor produced by AMD. It is different from any of the previous clone designs, since it uses its own motherboard design—actually related to the motherboards used for Alpha processors—rather than a Pentium motherboard. It also supports multiprocessor operation, and is claimed to have a very fast math co-processor, which should address any concerns about floating point performance. At the time of writing, Athlon processors are not available in bulk. However, they are being greeted enthusiastically by much of the Linux community and should make good high-performance workstations.

If you are interested in processor developments, you can find the latest specifications on these manufacturers' Web sites at http://www.intel.com/ and http://www.amd.com/, respectively.

There are also some independent Web sites which give news and reviews of recent hardware, for instance at http://www.tomshardware.com/.

PCS AS THEY SHOULD BE?

While many features of a modern PC are extremely sophisticated, there are still some significant pieces of legacy technology dating back to the days of the original i386 processors, or even earlier. The ISA bus, used by some expansion cards, is certainly past its prime for most applications.

Another part of the system that has a long history, and a tendency to cause problems, is the BIOS. This is a program which is present in Read Only Memory on any PC motherboard and is responsible for initializing the machine, starting the real operating system, and providing some basic input and output services. The DOS operating system relied heavily on the BIOS for everyday operation. But today, BIOS input/output support is inefficient, and sometimes problematic. Windows 95 bypasses the BIOS for many operations, and truly modern kernels such as Linux and Windows NT are very nearly independent of the BIOS once they have started. Nevertheless, the BIOS is still an unavoidable part of the current PC architecture. Some BIOS-related problems are discussed in later chapters.

Now, however, a change may be beginning. The most obvious example is SGI's Visual Workstation series of machines. Like many consumer PCs, these are based on Intel's Pentium II series of processors, but they use a very different motherboard architecture. The BIOS is gone as well; it has been replaced by a new piece of firmware that provides a more modern method of starting an operating system. Visual workstations are supplied running Windows NT, but, true to form, Linux developers soon got the kernel working. SGI has now committed to supporting Linux development, so Visual Workstation support should improve quite rapidly. SGI provides a Web site for anyone interested in running Linux on its hardware at http://www.linux.com/.

Visual workstations are high-end machines. But their basic architecture has many attractions, and now that SGI has broken the mold, other manufacturers may follow suit and offer more modern PCs.

Linux on the Move

Notebook PCs have traditionally been considered awkward targets for any operating system other than Windows. While this may be true for some older machines, most modern portables actually run Debian extremely well (as it happens, much of this book was written on an IBM Thinkpad running an almost entirely standard installation of the *potato* development version of Debian). In general, Linux can drive the basic hardware of most laptops with very little trouble. The biggest problems come from sound hardware (sound support is not always Linux's strongest point) and from internal modems (which are usually of the DSP WinModem type, and therefore need special drivers).

If you are interested in running Linux on a portable machine, it's worth looking at the Linux on Laptops Web site at `http://www.cs.utexas.edu/users/kharker/linux-laptop/`.

This site includes links to a number of useful Linux resources. There is also an impressive list of links to Web pages where users share their individual experiences installing Linux. As well as providing many useful tips for specific models, this list is also a useful starting point if you are buying a new laptop with a view of running Linux.

Other Architectures

The Linux kernel has been now been ported to most of the common processor architectures. Supported systems range from architectures such as Alpha, where support now compares favorably with the original Intel version, to unusual cases like MIPS, (for which support is still somewhat experimental). Debian releases are available for most architectures for which there is a reasonably established port of the kernel. Many of these ports are now very mature. Where appropriate, the kernel can take advantage of 64-bit processor architectures such as Alpha.

The main Debian installer programs work the same on all processor architecture. In general, the main place where installation on a non-Intel machine may differ significantly from the instructions given in Chapter 4, "A Basic Installation," is when booting the Linux kernel.

For Debian users, the `README` and `install.txt` files supplied along with the boot images for the particular distribution you are using should give some hints. For machines originally designed as workstations running a commercial UNIX system, the manufacturers normally provide some documentation describing the machine's *boot firmware*, which is the ROM-based program that you use to load the kernel.

There are pages of news relating to most of the non-Intel porting projects, which can be found at the main Debian Web site at `http://www.debian.org/`.

- **Alpha:** The Alpha/AXP architecture is probably the best-established port of the Linux kernel. There is a stable Debian port, and it should work well on just about any Alpha workstation. There are several boot firmware utilities seen on

Alpha systems. Most Linux/Alpha users use a tool called MILO to boot their systems, normally by starting it from the AlphaBIOS firmware. This process is described in the MILO-HOWTO document.

- **PowerPC:** The PowerPC chip is used primarily in Apple's PowerMac series of machines. Recent models are quite powerful, and make good Linux workstations. One point to be aware of is that the latest machines make extensive use of the USB interface. While Linux support for this does exist, it is still under development.

- **sparc:** Sparc processors are used in all but the earliest Sun hardware. There are actually two sparc architectures—an old 32-bit architecture, and a substantially redesigned 64-bit version, often called UltraSparc. Recent kernels support both architectures. Most sparc-based machines are single processor workstations, but there are also some large multiprocessor server machines, which also work well under Linux.

- **Motorola 680x0 (m68k):** The old Motorola architecture was used in many machines—the most important being Amigas, Atari machines, and the pre-PowerPC Apple Macintosh computers. Debian supports all three of these (although the Apple hardware support is rather limited). The PowerPC architecture is generally seen as the logical successor to the m68k series. While the m68k port was actually the first version of Linux to run on non-Intel processors, today it will primarily be of interest to people who want to get an old machine working as a low-spec UNIX system.

- **ARM:** ARM processors were originally used in machines built by the European company, Acorn. They are also found in Netwinder appliances, and are widely considered to be ideal for new generations of powerful ultraportable machines. There is an experimental Debian port to ARM-based machines, which is currently targeted primarily at the Netwinder.

- **Intel ia64:** Finally, one architecture that isn't supported at the moment, but which certainly will be in the future is the Intel current standard architecture. This architecture is often called the i386 architecture (Intel has retroactively named it ia32) and is now rather long in the tooth. It is due to be replaced with a new 64-bit architecture with many novel features.

In the long term, this spells the end for the current standard PC architecture, although it will certainly be a long time before it dies out completely. The first ia64 processors are due to ship in the year 2000, although they will initially be targeted only for server systems. A number of groups are working to ensure that the Linux will run on ia64 processors right from day one. It seems likely that a complete Debian distribution will be compiled soon after the processors appear on the market.

There are also a few architectures in which the Linux kernel will now run but Debian has not been compiled. The most notable of these is the MIPS architecture, used in SGI workstations. Nevertheless, Debian supports more architectures than any other distribution—in fact, it is one of only a handful of distributions that supports *any* non-Intel architecture.

Memory and Disk

It is difficult to give exact figures for the system resources required by a GNU/Linux system. It is supposedly still possible to boot a standard Linux kernel on a machine with only 4MB of memory, and certainly with 8MB it can run reasonably well, if you only want a few simple tools. How much more than this you require depends on your applications. In practice, if you are going to be using a graphical user interface and some windowed applications, 32MB is probably a reasonable starting place. But adding more than that can improve performance considerably.

If, after getting your Debian system running, you think that your machine may be short of memory, try using the free command to view details of current memory usage. A little care is needed when interpreting this information. For instance, on a lightly loaded 96MB machine, typing free at the command prompt gives the following results:

```
              total      used      free    shared   buffers    cached Mem:
              94852     93424      1428     39460     46652     23868
-/+ buffers/cache:       22904     71948
Swap:        130748       180    130568
```

The first line shows that virtually all of the machine's memory is being used for something. However, this is misleading—the Linux kernel considers any memory that applications aren't currently using as fair game for caching recently accessed areas of your hard disk. This can significantly improve apparent disk performance. But if an application needs more space, all this memory can be quickly reclaimed.

A more realistic reflection of memory use appears in the second line, which counts memory used for disk caches as free. This shows that this particular machine has plenty of RAM to spare. The final line gives details of swap space—virtual memory stored on the hard disk. This virtual memory will be used to a large extent only if the machine comes close to running out of main memory.

One point to remember is that the performance of any modern computer is strongly dependent on cache RAM: special high speed memory devices which store copies of recently accessed areas of main memory. While it may be physically possible to include large amounts of RAM, many older Pentium motherboards can only use the cache for accesses to the first 64MB of physical memory. This can sometimes lead to a surprising situation whereby adding extra memory actually reduces performance, at least for certain applications. If in doubt, check your motherboard documentation before adding memory. More modern Pentium motherboards will usually allow caching of substantially more memory. Pentium II processors use a rather different cache design, and support up to 512MB of memory, irrespective of the motherboard that you use.

Disk space is another area where requirements can vary dramatically. With a little experience it's possible to install a small Debian system—more than enough to work as a simple print server, for instance—on a 50MB hard disk partition, and still have some space left over. On the other hand, if you want a reasonably comprehensive worksta-tion installation plus some room for experimentation, 500MB of free space is probably a sensible minimum, and having a full gigabyte could make life more comfortable. Additional guidelines for allocating disk space for Linux, together with instructions for repartitioning your drives, are included in Chapter 3, "Getting Ready—Disk Space."

CD-ROM Drives

CD-ROM drives have been ubiquitous in new PCs for several years, and most people will be carrying out their first Debian installation from a CD-ROM distribution. Virtually all CD-ROMs found today are IDE devices (or, more accurately, ATAPI, which is a hybrid system that uses SCSI-like protocols on an IDE bus). There are still some SCSI CD-ROMs around, but they are rarely seen in new computers. ATAPI devices may make for a slightly easier Debian installation.

Older machines may be fitted with some other kind of CD-ROM drive—when the tech-nology was still quite new, there were many non-ATAPI systems that were used to attach a CD to the IDE bus. A lot of these *will* work, but you will generally not be able to boot Linux directly from the CD.

DVD-ROMs

DVD-ROM drives work fine under Linux. But at the moment they are only really use-ful for reading normal CD-ROMs. Most DVDs currently available contain video data in a proprietary format, and decoding software that runs under Linux is currently not available.

Generic data DVDs also present a problem. Many of them store data using the new UDF filesystem, which is currently not supported by the Linux kernel. At the time of writing, there is some experimental UDF support code available, which will probably be part of the standard kernel by the time DVDs become a common medium for gen-eral data distribution.

CD Writers

Unlike most common pieces of hardware, CD writers are normally controlled by a sep-arate program rather than by a driver built into the kernel. The cdrecord package, included in the Debian distribution, can drive most common models, both SCSI and IDE. SCSI-based devices may be slightly easier to use. Internally, the IDE writers are actually identical to their SCSI counterparts, but they use ATAPI rather than normal SCSI interfaces. To use them, you need the ide-scsi kernel module, which should be installed with Debian.

There are a number of graphical packages that act as frontends for cdrecord and a number of other tools that provide a friendly environment for assembling both audio and data CDs (see Figure 2.1). Several of these tools can be found in the otherosfs section of the Debian distribution.

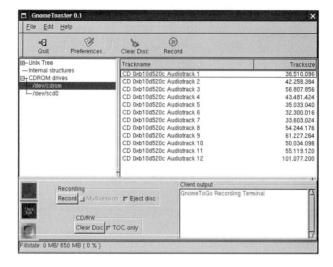

Figure 2.1

GToaster is one of several packages that offers drag-and-drop assembly of compilation CDs.

Other Expansion Devices

While Linux supports most common PC-based hardware, support for expansion cards and other devices is sometimes a little weaker. This is due largely to the sheer number of different devices available—the Linux kernel, plus associated packages, include support for a vast array of products, but there are still gaps in the support. Problems normally arise with devices that are very old, very new, or are rather obscure.

The rest of this chapter tries to list some of the most important devices that might cause problems for the typical Debian user. This discussion is certainly not exhaustive. Some devices are excluded because they are generally trouble-free. Just about any modern mouse (and many other kinds of pointing devices) should work fine. Printers, too, are very rarely the cause of hardware problems—instructions for setting up a printer for easy use under Debian can be found in Chapter 8, "Advanced Configuration."

In the last few years, an increasing number of hardware manufacturers have shown at least some willingness to accept that Linux-based operating systems now have a significant market share. In recognition of this, you can now find information about Linux compatibility on company Web sites, or even on the packaging of some products. If you're buying new hardware, statements of Linux support are a useful reassurance. You should also think about supporting companies that support Linux, in preference to organizations that go on thinking that Windows is the only operating system out there.

At the time of writing, the Linux community is starting to switch over from 2.0 kernels (used in Debian versions up to 2.1) to the 2.2 series (which will be included in the next release). Support for some kinds of hardware—especially newer devices—is better with 2.2 kernels, and some users will benefit from upgrading. It is possible to run a 2.2-series kernel on a standard Debian 2.1 installation, if you upgrade it manually. Instructions for upgrading kernels appear in Appendix A.

For many classes of devices, there are no totally comprehensive lists of supported models. If in doubt, it's sometimes worth taking a look at the source package for the kernel. If you install it as described in Appendix A, you can then browse the main kernel options, including all the devices which are supported, by typing

`make menuconfig`

If you're working in a windowed environment, you may prefer to see a more graphical view of kernel options (see Figure 2.2) by typing

`make xconfig`

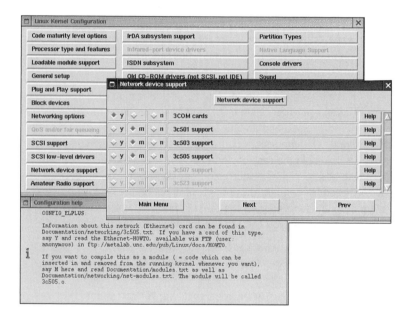

Figure 2.2

Delving into source code is sometimes seen as the scary side of an open-source operating system. But browsing the configuration options for the Linux kernel can be an easy way to determine if your hardware is supported.

Modern desktop PCs accept two types of expansion cards—old ISA cards and the newer, faster, PCI standard. As well as the speed advantage, PCI cards have a major advantage because they are not prone to conflicts with system resources. ISA hardware is now becoming less common, and Intel appears to be trying to phase out support for the system in future motherboard designs.

Portable PCs use credit-card sized PC cards (the older name, PCMCIA, is still widely used). Linux PC card support is provided by a separate package—but this is automatically included in the Debian install procedure if it is needed. A list of supported PC cards can be found on the home page for the pcmcia-cs package at http://hyper.stanford.edu/HyperNews/get/pcmcia/home.html.

MAGIC IN THE NUMBERS: USING ISA CARDS

In any computing system, there must be some mechanism by which the processor and the peripheral hardware can communicate. Each expansion card in a computer uses certain communication resources, each with a unique number. For most purposes, these can just be considered *magic numbers* that happen to be necessary for the computer to work. Ideally, when a computer starts up, all cards should have their resources set up automatically. This ideal situation is sometimes called *plug-and-play* (PnP). Modern architectures, such as PCI, are designed right from the beginning to allow PnP.

The ISA architecture, however, is not inherently PnP. In recent years, attempts have been made to retrofit PnP to the old ISA bus but, especially for Linux users, ISA PnP can often create more problems than it solves.

The ISA bus allows three kinds of communication resource: shared memory areas, interrupt numbers (often called IRQs), and DMA channels. Most ISA devices use a shared memory region and an IRQ, while only some (notably sound cards) need a DMA channel. The important point is that each device in the computer *must* use unique resources. In the case of non-PnP ISA cards, this means manually setting up the card to ensure that its resources do not clash with existing devices. This is normally achieved by manually moving link-jumpers on the card, or by using a configuration program supplied with the card. To find out which resources are already in use in your computer, you can use the following commands:

```
cat /proc/ioports      # List shared memory
cat /proc/interrupts   # List allocated interrupt lines
cat /proc/dma          # List allocated ISA DMA channels.
```

The problems really begin when you use newer ISA cards that claim to support PnP. In some cases, it's still possible to manually jump or configure these cards to use specific resources—if so, this is often the easiest solution.

If you really *must* use ISA PnP devices, you can try telling your BIOS that you don't have a PnP operating system. In this case, it should allocate resources to PnP cards itself, and set them to an active state. If this fails, there is a package called isapnptools, supplied with the Debian distribution, that can get most PnP devices working. But this can be a very technically demanding job.

In conclusion, the ISA bus is obsolete technology, and it is likely to be phased out completely in the near future. If you have a modern PCI-based machine, given the choice it is almost always best to buy PCI expansion cards, since they are truly PnP. If you're installing Debian on an older machine that has an ISA bus, stick to old pre-PnP cards, or cards that can be manually configured.

Graphics Cards

For most users, the ability to drive a monitor (or liquid crystal panel display) is essential. This means either a graphics card or (in the case of laptops and some recent low-end desktops) a video chipset on the motherboard. Old machines used ISA-based graphics cards, but these are now very rare. Almost all cards today plug into a PCI slot or, increasingly commonly, into an AGP (advanced graphics port) slot. AGP is an interface similar to PCI but it is optimized specifically for high-performance graphics cards.

Simply running Linux is generally not a problem with almost any PC graphics card: The basic text-only console that the kernel provides when it first starts up requires only VGA support in the graphics card. This has been universal for many years.

Graphics support for running windowed applications is normally provided not by the kernel but by a separate application called an X server. (The X Window system is introduced in Chapter 6, "The First Steps in Debian.") Debian installations almost always use an X server from the XFree86 project. These X servers support a very wide variety of graphics cards and chipsets. So long as you use an up-to-date version of XFree86, most modern graphics cards will work.

If you have a *recent* graphics card that is currently unsupported, you might like to try an alternative method of running the X Window system, by using the Framebuffer system found in recent kernels. This provides limited support for any graphics card that implements the VESA 2.0 standard. If you are unlucky enough to have an unsupported graphics card, look at the Framebuffer-HOWTO at http://www.tahallah. demon.co.uk/.

Where XFree86 does currently lag behind the state of the art is when supporting accelerated 3D features in modern graphics cards. To date, this lack of support has restricted Linux's acceptance as a platform for gaming and certain specialist applications. However, 3D support may improve dramatically in the near future, especially with the forthcoming release of XFree86 4.0.

SCSI Controllers

SCSI was originally used primarily as a mechanism for connecting hard disks to computers. In today's desktop computer market, this is actually a rather rare application of the technology—while SCSI drives are still thought to perform a little better than their IDE counterparts, the price difference is rarely justifiable. SCSI hard disks are, however, still common for server machines.

Most common SCSI cards are supported well, from old ones to new models. Think twice before using an old ISA device though. Not only will you suffer from the problems of configuration, but performance will also suffer. The only real use for an ISA SCSI card is in an old, pre-PCI machine.

In modern desktop computers, SCSI cards are most often found driving devices such as scanners and CD writers. This generally isn't as demanding as running the machine's main hard disk. Even so, it's generally best to avoid very cheap or free cards supplied with devices such as scanners—these are often ISA cards, and lead to configuration difficulties and poor performance. And they may not be supported at all. If you want to use any SCSI device, it's worth investing in a good basic PCI controller card.

Ethernet Adapters

Linux is very strong as a network operating system, and so it is not surprising that support for Ethernet adapters is generally excellent. For desktop machines there is a choice between ISA and PCI cards—as usual, PCI cards are generally less trouble.

There is a wide range of network cards available, all differing considerably in price. Among the cheapest are clones of the old Novell NE2000 card, which are now available in both ISA and PCI variants. These cards work well under Linux, and are ideal if you want to set up a small home network. However, more expensive cards do bring benefits in reliability and performance, and are worthwhile for serious network users, especially if you're setting up a server machine. The best way to verify that a specific network card is supported without actually trying it is to look at the kernel configuration options.

Laptop users now have a number of different Ethernet PC cards to choose from. Many of these work fine with the pcmcia-cs package, but check the compatibility list first, and be a little cautious if you are offered an unbranded card.

Sound Cards

Of all the common pieces of PC hardware, sound cards are probably the most awkward for Linux users. It has been suggested that this might be partially due to Linus himself not being especially interested in sound support.

Currently, the sound support built into the kernel is called OSS/Linux (for Open Sound System). When it works, it can perform quite well. However, only a relatively limited selection of cards are supported, and most of these are old models. There is a commercial release of OSS that supports more cards—but at a price. If you are interested in trying the commercial OSS, look for it at http://www.opensound.com/.

Another alternative is offered by the Advanced Linux Sound Architecture (ALSA) project. This is an entirely free effort to create a new sound infrastructure and driver set, which may eventually replace OSS in the standard kernel. Recent versions of Debian include the main ALSA components as standard Debian packages, which make for easy installation. They provide a new programmer's interface to the sound system (although compatibility with OSS is maintained if you need it). If you're having trouble getting your sound card working (especially if it's a recent design), it could be worth looking at the list of supported cards on the ALSA Web site at http://www.alsa-project.org/.

Modems

Modems fall into two classes—internal and external. External modems, which plug into the serial port, need no special drivers and thus cause no problems under Linux. Although they may clutter up your desk, external modems are always a safe bet.

In the case of internal modems, the situation is a little more complex. Many of these, especially the ISA-based models, are essentially identical to their external counterparts, and communicate with the computer via a serial port controller chip on the card. Internal modems simply appear to the system as an extra serial port, and also need no extra driver. These are the only common ISA-based devices which can really be recommended for use in a new Linux machine.

You may, however, need to manually configure the kernel's serial driver to identify your internal modem (see the sidebar on ISA cards). For instance, for a modem card that has been manually set to use interrupt line 5 and a shared memory region at 0x03e8, you can configure the serial driver (while logged on as the root user) with the following command:

```
setserial /dev/ttyS2 port 0x03e8 irq 5
```

Note that /dev/ttyS2 is a UNIX device name corresponding to a serial port (in this case, the device which would normally be called COM3 under DOS). The real meaning of these device names is explained in later chapters. To make this a permanent setting, edit the configuration file:

```
/etc/init.d/serial
```

or (under Debian versions later than 2.1)

```
/etc/serial.conf
```

Some recent internal modem cards—and almost all the built-in modems for laptop machines—work in a different manner. DSP modems (often called WinModems, although this term is slightly misleading, and is actually a trademark referring to one specific brand) are simpler, and hence often cheaper, than real modems, but require software support from a complex driver. So far, the manufacturers have been reluctant to release the specifications that would allow people to write drivers for these devices. For now, they are indeed tied to Windows. With the increasing popularity and commercial recognition of Linux, it is possible that this situation could change in the future, but for now DSP modems of any type should be avoided.

Laptop users can choose from a variety of modems available as PC cards. Again, some emulate normal serial ports, while others are of the DSP type—the former are the ones to choose.

Scanners

Many modern scanner models are supported by the SANE package, distributed with Debian. This allows scanning either from the command line or (with the xscanimage package) in a graphical environment (see Figure 2.3). There is a compatibility list on the SANE home page at http://www.mostang.com/sane/.

Current scanners tend to connect to the computer either by SCSI or via the parallel (printer) port. The majority of supported scanners are connected via the SCSI port, although SANE does also support a few parallel scanners—but check before you buy.

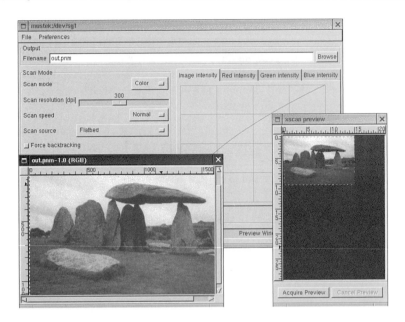

Figure 2.3

The SANE package offers good support for many modern scanners.

Some older scanners—usually handheld models—used dedicated interface cards rather than a standard port, and these are generally not usable under Linux. Stand-alone drivers are available for a few of these, but they are normally old, and can be primitive.

Interfaces of the Future

In the last few years, a number of new standards have emerged for connecting computers to peripheral devices. The trend seems to be a strong move away from monolithic computers that have to be plugged together, carefully set up, and then left that way. The PC card interface used by laptop computers is already hot-pluggable—you can insert and remove cards while the computer is switched on, and expect it to automatically reconfigure. Within the next few years, more and more devices will be connected using new, flexible interfaces.

USB

Universal Serial Bus (USB) is a high-speed serial interface proposed several years ago as a convenient method for attaching many devices, from keyboards to scanners, to new computers. The standard has been designed around a concept of hot-pluggable devices. Most new PCs now have a USB socket, but USB devices are still relatively rare. This is now changing, with USB devices being supplied with recent Apple computers, and also with the SGI Visual workstations. The Linux USB support code is currently still under development, and is expected to merge into the 2.3 development series of kernels.

The USB code will support some common devices—notably keyboards and mice—as standard, but additional drivers will be required for more specialized devices, such as scanners and digital cameras.

IrDA

An even more dramatic example of dynamically connectable hardware is the set of communications protocols specified by the Infrared Data Association (IrDA). Infrared transceivers are becoming increasingly common—they are now found on the majority of laptops and palmtop portable computers, and can be fitted to desktop machines. Infrared support is also found on many other pieces of hardware, notably printers and high-end mobile phones.

Preliminary IrDA support for many devices is present in 2.2-series Linux kernels, and is improving continually. It is possible to set up wireless network links between IrDA-capable PCs, communicate with palmtop devices, and print from laptop machines without needing a cable. If you have some IrDA-capable devices and want to try them out, take a look at the Linux-IrDA project home page at `http://www.cs.uit.no/~dagb/irda/`.

This site includes a comprehensive IrDA-HOWTO document that describes all of the various sub-protocols used to communicate with specific types of devices, and gives advice on setting up your hardware.

Firewire (IEEE 1394)

At a simple level, firewire acts a little like USB—but faster. This standard is, for instance, ideal for supporting hot-pluggable hard disks. Firewire devices are not yet common, and as yet, there is no established Linux support. But work is underway to change this. If you're interested in projects that are working to support firewire, or any other new hardware technology, you might like to look through archives of the Linux-kernel mailing list, the main forum of kernel developers. For more details, see Chapter 11, "And Finally—Welcome to the Community."

Summary

This chapter covers the most important pieces of hardware that can be used with a Debian GNU/Linux system, and gives some links that you may find useful for obtaining up-to-the-minute information on the Linux compatibility of specific devices. You might want to refer back to this chapter once your first Debian installation is complete for help in resolving any hardware problems you encounter, or for advice on purchasing new Linux-compatible hardware.

If you are happy that your computer base system is ready to run Linux, you can now proceed to the next chapter, which covers hard disk partitioning. You will then be ready to carry out the installation itself.

CHAPTER 3

Getting Ready—Disk Space

In this chapter, you begin the Debian installation process in earnest. For many would-be Linux users, the need to repartition an existing hard disk can be the most intimidating part of the whole installation process. If you are installing on an existing machine, you *may* need to completely reformat your hard disk. But this is the worst-case scenario, and there are a number of possible methods that can allow you to avoid this scenario altogether.

This chapter also covers some basic ideas about how Linux stores files on disk partitions, and explains the most important landmarks in the directory structure that will be created when you install Debian. File systems are a fundamental part of the Linux kernel, so most of the ideas in this chapter actually apply to any Linux-based distribution.

Most first-time Debian installers will want to add GNU/Linux as a second operating system to a machine that is already in use—probably running Windows. If you have a separate computer that you can devote entirely to your new Debian installation, life will become somewhat easier, but running a separate computer is not always practical.

Before going any further, an oft-repeated, but almost as frequently ignored, piece of advice: Whatever you're doing with your computer, keep a backup of any important files. Even if you can avoid a complete reformat of your hard disk, you will still need to modify your hard disk partition tables before you can install any Linux-based system.

The large size of modern hard disks means that backing up data to floppy disks is rarely an attractive, or even practical, prospect. But there is a selection of removable mass-storage devices, some of which are now quite cheap. Even though installing Debian isn't a particularly dangerous operation, there are many ways in which data can be lost, whether you are installing a new operating system or using the computer normally. If you value your data at all, back it up now. You never know when you'll be glad that you did.

Introduction to Disks

Like any UNIX system, Debian gives most hardware devices names. These names are not just meaningless labels: They actually represent special files that can be read and written to directly, although as a normal user you will probably have little cause to access these files. But it is useful to understand the names of the devices you will be dealing with throughout the installation process, as well as how they are assigned.

All modern consumer PCs use some form of the ATA (IDE) interface to control the hard disks and CD-ROM devices. Each IDE controller can drive two devices, the master and the slave. If only one device is installed on the controller, it is always the master. The master device attached to the first controller is known to Linux systems as /dev/hda, and the slave is /dev/hdb. Standard PC-type motherboards almost always have two IDE controllers: devices on the second controller are /dev/hdc and /dev/hdd. A typical machine's hard disk is /dev/hda and the CD-ROM drive is either /dev/hdb or /dev/hdc, depending on the cabling inside the machine.

On normal desktop machines, SCSI hard disks are now relatively rare, but they are still used on high-specification servers. If you have any fitted, Linux allocates them names of the form /dev/sdx, where x is a letter allocated in the order that drives are detected when the system starts up. SCSI CD-ROM drives and CD writers have their own naming scheme: The first one detected is /dev/scd0.

A hard disk can be split into several partitions, each of which can be formatted separately. This standard method of partitioning disks makes it possible for Linux and some other operating system to coexist peacefully on the same physical device. You sometimes encounter partitioning even on a machine that only runs DOS or Windows. It is possible to have more than one DOS-formatted partition, in which case these are automatically detected and assigned letters. A single physical hard disk with two partitions would typically appear to the user as the logical disk drives C: and D:.

Linux, on the other hand, does not adopt the DOS concept of drive letters. Instead, partitions are explicitly mounted, which makes them part of a single directory hierarchy called the virtual file system. However, each partition on a disk, irrespective of its format, does have its own device name. This name consists of the name of the disk drive as a whole, followed by a number representing the specific partition.

The traditional partitioning mechanism allows for up to four partitions on a disk, referred to as primary partitions. For the first IDE drive, these would be named /dev/hda1 to /dev/hda4. But if you want more than four partitions, one of the primary partitions can be a special extended partition. The extended partition has its own partition table, and can contain additional partitions. Linux numbers these from five upward, even if you have fewer than four primary partitions. They are called logical partitions, although they are just as real as primary partitions. For most purposes there is no practical difference between the two, and you can create whichever type is most convenient.

The one case where you will definitely need to use a primary partition is as the C: drive from which you will be booting a Windows system. In principle, it is possible to place a Debian installation entirely in logical partitions. There is, however, a slight complication when installing the Linux loader program on such a system. The Debian installer detects this case and handles it automatically. Nevertheless, many users still prefer to use a primary partition as the root partition used to boot Linux.

Types of Disk Partition

Most operating systems use their own formats for disk partitions. For current Linux systems, the native format is the Second Extended file system (widely abbreviated as ext2). This format supports all the common features of modern UNIX file systems: the ability to use long names, and the ability to associate user IDs and access permission details with each file. It also gives generally good performance, both in terms of speed and use of disk space, for a wide variety of common applications.

Other operating systems have their own formats. For instance, MS DOS and all the pre-NT Windows systems use variants of the FAT file system. They all understand the old FAT16 format, which dates back to the early days of DOS. The FAT16 format is now considered very inefficient, especially when used with large disks. Remember that it was designed at a time when 20 megabytes seemed spacious! Windows 98 adds support for a newer, and more efficient, format called FAT32, which is used by default on at least some pre-installed Windows 98 machines, especially when a large hard disk is supplied. FAT32 support was also present in the final release of Windows 95: Note that there are usually several 'maintenance' releases for each major Windows release, and some of these contain significant new features.

Recent Linux kernels, including the version supplied with Debian 2.1, can read both variants of FAT. Don't worry about reports that only FAT16 file systems can be mounted; this is true only for older kernels.

The FAT file systems were originally designed with filenames limited to an eight-character name and a three-character extension (8.3 format). As of Windows 95, an extension called VFAT provides support for longer filenames. When you are mounting a Windows 95 partition under Linux, it is worth specifying that VFAT is used, since otherwise you will see the rather cryptic shortened form of any long filenames. There are more hints on Debian-Windows file exchange in Chapter 8, "Advanced Configuration."

Windows NT can access FAT16 partitions, but more often uses its own file system format, NTFS. There is experimental support for accessing NTFS volumes in recent Linux kernels, but it is currently not recommended for normal users. If you want an easy way of transferring data between Debian and NT installations on the same system, create a FAT partition that can be accessed by both systems. Other operating systems— including other UNIX-like systems—all have their own formats. An ever-increasing number of these are supported, at least in a limited read-only mode, by the latest versions of Linux.

There is also one file system type that you will never use on hard disks, but that is important nonetheless. Virtually all data CD-ROMs use the ISO 9660 file system, which is optimized exclusively for read operations. There is no way to write to an ISO 9660 file system. If you want to create one—usually useful only when you have a CD writer—use the mkisofs tool. This tool takes a normal directory of files and assembles them into a complete file system, which can then be written directly onto a CD.

MORE LINUX FILE SYSTEMS?

Since early in the history of Linux, the ext2 file system has been the standard for almost all installations—it will certainly be what you use in your first Debian system. But there are several alternatives emerging that might eventually replace ext2. That said, you can be sure that good ext2fs support will remain in the Linux kernel for a long time. None of the file systems described here are included in standard Linux distributions such as Debian. Initially, they will be used only by kernel developers for testing purposes, and by system administrators who need very high performance file systems. But at least some of them will gradually filter into widespread use over the next few years.

The first possible replacement is being worked on by some of the main Linux kernel developers, and is a logical extension of ext2. It will probably go by the rather unimaginative name of ext3. The main feature of ext3 is *journaling*, a technology that prevents disks from being left in an inconsistent state when there is a major system failure, such as an unexpected power loss. There are also likely to be some useful performance improvements. You can expect ext3 support to be merged into the Linux 2.3 development series.

Two other new Linux file systems also offer journaling. XFS is an advanced file system originally developed for the Irix operating system. The developers, SGI, have recently offered it to Linux users. It is not yet certain how XFS will be supplied to Linux users, but it could eventually become an attractive alternative. Another up-and-coming system is reiserfs, an experimental file system design that could offer big performance improvements, especially on partitions used to store a large number of small files. The reiserfs system is already attracting interest from system administrators, and could become a option for everyday Debian users in the near future.

Geometric Concerns

The size of a hard disk is the product of a number of values, which together make up the disk's geometry. Each of the data storage surfaces of the disk (called *heads*) is divided into concentric rings, variously called *cylinders* or *tracks*. The tracks are in turn subdivided into *sectors*. A typical disk might have a geometry as shown here:

Cylinders	7944
Heads	16
Sectors/cylinder	63
Bytes/sector	512
Total	4,099,866,624 bytes

(or, depending on whose definition of a gigabyte you use, somewhere around 4GB). Note that the number of heads, sectors, and bytes/sector are fixed for virtually any modern IDE drive—it is the number of cylinders that varies.

With today's operating systems, the exact geometry of a hard disk would be irrelevant were it not for one unfortunate fact: When an operating system is first started, the kernel must be loaded from the disk using the code present in the machine's BIOS. The BIOS interfaces are very old, and are able to read data only from the first 1024 cylinders of a disk. This doesn't actually prevent the use of large disks—once a Linux-based system is up and running, it accesses the disk drive hardware independently of the BIOS. But to boot the system in the first place, the kernel code, which is normally stored on your root partition, *must* be present somewhere in the first 1024 cylinders of the disk.

This is particularly serious when you realize that standard IDE disks are limited to 16 heads and 63 sectors per track—this restricts the bootable area of the disk to slightly less than half a gigabyte. Fortunately, modern BIOSes offer an option called *logical block addressing* (LBA), which hides the real geometry of the disk and instead creates an alternative logical geometry where up to 256 heads are allowed. So long as this option is enabled (as it almost certainly will be for any machine manufactured in the last few years), the geometry problem disappears for disks up to 8GB.

If you are uncertain as to whether LBA mode is active, try rebooting your machine and calling up the BIOS setup screen. There will normally be a section that shows the complete geometry of each disk, and specifies whether LBA is in use. Alternatively, just boot from a Debian rescue disk (described in Chapter 4, "A Basic Installation"), start the installer, and run the `cfdisk` program, as explained in the latter part of this chapter. If this process reports more than 16 heads, the disk is in LBA mode. So long as `cfdisk` reports fewer than 1024 cylinders, you have nothing to worry about.

But with disk sizes increasing constantly, even the current LBA support cannot prevent booting problems from occurring with some setups. If you have a very large disk that you want to share between Windows and Debian, you will probably want a partitioning scheme similar to the one shown in Figure 3.1. This scheme uses two Windows partitions, C: and D:, and two separate partitions that make up different parts of the complete Debian file system. The critical feature is that both Windows and Linux boot from partitions below the 1024 cylinder boundary.

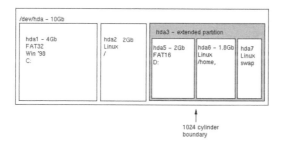

Figure 3.1

An example partitioning scheme that makes the most of the large hard disks now commonly available.

Room to Breathe

Before beginning a Debian installation, it's worth spending some time thinking about how much disk space you are going to devote to Linux. The easy answer is "as much as you can," and there are good reasons to commend this answer. Debian is not a small distribution—it is designed to provide a wide range of tools to suit all kinds of users. Even though it is possible to set up a Debian installation that uses very little space, there are a lot of non-essential packages that you'll probably want to at least try at some point. Therefore, it is worth leaving some space to play with.

As a practical guideline, you can take 500MB as a sensible minimum for a first Linux installation. This minimum enables you to have a graphical desktop environment and some major applications, and still leaves some room for trying out a selection of the more unusual packages, as well as for keeping your own files.

The type of work that you will do with Debian also has some effect. For the programmer, there are a huge range of development tools that you might want to at least consider, so extra space will come in handy. Similarly, if you are interested in serious image-manipulation work using tools such as *The Gimp*, disk space could vanish rather rapidly.

If you are planning to build any software from source code, you will also need to allow a lot of space for the source code and intermediate files in the compilation process. The Linux 2.2 kernel source, newly unpacked, weighs in at around 60MB. Today, most people can make do with a pre-compiled kernel, but it is occasionally useful to build your own—see Appendix A, "Kernel Management." Source code for application software can be big too. If you're interested in following the open-source development of Netscape's latest Web browser product, you'll need several hundred megabytes for your copy of the source code and build files.

Note that the core GNU/Linux system actually takes only a small fraction of the space recommended for a full Debian installation. A machine that's going to sit in the corner of an office and act as a server often needs far fewer packages installed and therefore (depending on how many user files you are expecting to store on it), may need less disk space.

But if you're new to Linux, it's best to start with a comprehensive workstation installation with plenty of disk space to spare. Once you're happy using the dselect tool (see Chapter 5, "Making Your Selection") and are familiar with the main Debian packages you need, you'll have no trouble setting up more installations that meet your specific requirements.

Swap Space

Like any other modern operating system, the memory management system in the Linux kernel can move data out to disk when physical RAM is running short. This process is called *swapping*. It sometimes also goes by the name *virtual memory*, although this is not entirely correct, since the swapping mechanism is only one aspect of the kernel's complex virtual memory subsystem.

Windows normally uses a regular file for its swap space. This file is created automatically and many users aren't even aware that it exists. Linux can also swap to a file, but it is more common to use a dedicated hard disk partition—the whole partition is treated as though it is a single file. This gives a performance advantage, since that swapped data can be sent straight to the hard disk rather than having to pass through the file system code first. Debian prompts you to activate a swap partition during the standard install procedure, and for your first installation, you should always do this. If, later on, you really want to experiment with unusual swap configurations, read the manual pages for the mkswap and swapon commands.

If there's any chance that you're likely to do memory-intensive work, it's worth allowing a reasonable amount of swap space—modern programs tend to work on the assumption that they will never run out of memory. The Linux 2.0 kernel, used by Debian versions up to 2.1, limits swap partitions to a maximum size of 128MB. If you have a large hard disk and limited memory, it may well be worth creating a swap partition of that size. The Linux 2.2 kernel, and future versions of Debian, remove that limitation. If you expect to compile large programs, or deal with huge data files, you might want to create an even bigger swap partition.

The Virtual File System

Once a UNIX-based computer is up and running, you do not directly access your hard disk partitions by their names. Instead, all your files, irrespective of the physical device they are stored on, appear in a single virtual file system.

When the kernel first starts up, it identifies one partition as the *root* of the file system. The top level directory on this partition becomes the directory /, the root of the whole hierarchy. But it is then possible to add extra partitions by a process called *mounting*, whereby a (normally empty) directory, called the *mount point*, is replaced by the top level directory from a new partition. Often, several file systems are mounted automatically at boot time, but it is also possible to mount more at any time.

This is true even for removable media such as floppy disks and CD-ROMs. It is common to create a directory—often called /v—that contains convenient mount points for any removable media you use.

As a simple example, to mount a DOS FAT-format disk in the first floppy drive (/dev/fd0) and make its contents appear in the directory /v/floppy, you use the following command:

```
mount -t vfat /dev/fd0 /v/floppy
```

If you use floppies often, don't worry about the length of this command—methods for simplifying the mounting process are described in Chapter 8. Once you are finished with a file system you have manually mounted, you can reverse the process with a command such as

```
umount /v/floppy
```

The Debian Directory Hierarchy

On Windows systems, it is normal to simply create personal files and directories in the root directory of a hard disk partition. There is just one top-level directory (normally C:\Windows) that contains all the system files. UNIX systems, on the other hand, have well-defined standard directory structures. Each user who has an account on the machine will create personal files in a special home directory.

All modern Linux distributions broadly follow the directory structure set out in a document called the File system Hierarchy Standard (FHS). Debian generally follows FHS quite closely, while other distributions may differ in some ways. Once you have learned your way round Debian's directory structure, you will normally have few problems with any other, but do be prepared for subtle differences. Some of the main directories are listed in Figure 3.2.

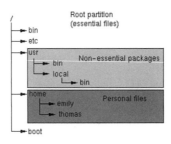

Figure 3.2

Simplified view of a standard Debian file system structure. Note how the directory structure has been split across three disk partitions—you don't have to use multiple partitions, but such arrangements can make it easier to recover important data after a system failure, and are favored by experienced UNIX administrators.

Perhaps the most important standard directories are those called bin and sbin. These directories are where all the main commands and programs of the GNU/Linux system are stored. Commands that normal users are likely to use are found in bin directories, whereas sbin is normally reserved for system-management tools.

The bin and sbin directories in the root directory are reserved for only the most essential tools. Other top-level directories include /etc (contains system-wide configuration files) and /var (used mainly for temporary files—outgoing email messages are queued up here, for instance). Finally, another top level directory, /usr, contains less vital files. For instance, an application program such as a word processor is normally installed in the non-essential programs directory, /usr/bin.

There are also a number of additional standard directories that are important to the functioning of a GNU/Linux system. Notable among these are the /lib directory, which contains shared pieces of code used by many programs, and the /boot directory, where files related to the initial loading of the kernel are stored.

Users' home directories can be placed anywhere in the hierarchy. But unless you have a very large number of users, you will probably want to follow the Debian standard policy of giving each user a home in the /home top-level directory. The adduser tool (see Chapter 6, "The First Steps in Debian") normally creates new home directories in this location.

While personal work files almost always belong in your home directory, it *is* sometimes useful to create new top-level directories. In particular, you will probably want to create mount points for accessing your CD-ROM and floppy disk drives, and perhaps also your Windows partition. This process is discussed further in Chapter 8.

Arranging Linux Partitions

A typical UNIX system for personal use will normally follow a partition structure similar to the one shown in Figure 3.2. But the partitioning scheme is optional—in many situations it is entirely possible to hold the whole directory structure on a single partition. This is often a reasonable option for the first-time Linux user. Nevertheless, there are good reasons for using multiple partitions.

The first reason why you might need to split your data is to overcome the 1024 cylinder limitation when installing on a large disk. It is only necessary to have one partition (almost always the root partition) lying below the 1024 cylinder boundary. Other partitions that make up your complete file system can be elsewhere on the disk, or even on a different device.

The other—and more traditional—reason for multiple partitions is safety. In particular, having user home directories on a separate partition allows you to be sure that they won't be touched during an upgrade. It is possible to perform a complete new install of Debian, or even some other Linux distribution, and then remount your /home partition safe in the knowledge that all personal files will still be there. For a personal machine, you may only have one user directory under /home, or perhaps a handful for family or friends. But for server installations, there are often hundreds of users to deal with. In this case, /home will probably have a whole hard disk, or perhaps even a large disk array, to itself.

The same goes if you install a lot of packages that aren't part of the standard Debian distribution. These customarily go in directories in the /usr/local hierarchy—which is never touched by normal Debian packages—and some users choose to mount a separate partition there.

In conclusion, it *is* possible to use just a single data partition (plus the standard swap partition, of course). If you are a first-time Linux user and are unsure about how you're going to be using the system, this configuration is often the simplest option. This configuration also prevents you from running out of space on one partition while still having plenty to spare on another.

If you are serious about using Debian, and have a reasonable amount of disk space to spare, it's worth creating a separate /home partition. Remember that this will only contain your personal files: All the program files will be elsewhere, so unless you routinely work with large files (images, for instance), you will probably want a /home partition which is rather smaller than your main partition. For the experienced user, using just a small root partition (150MB is usually more than adequate for a home machine) and placing /usr on a separate partition is also a good move. This leaves only system-wide configuration data and essential tools on the root partition, and makes it easier to repair the system if a disk partition is corrupted—due to a power failure while writing to a disk, for instance.

Once you have been using UNIX systems for a while, you will get a feel for the best way to partition a disk drive. If you are running a large server machine, you will probably want to take a look at the /var directory. On a typical home machine, this will usually be quite small. But since /var is the standard location for email spools and Web page data, it could grow dramatically on some server installations. In this case, you might want to mount a new partition on /var. But it is best to avoid such complications until you are familiar with the day-to-day workings of a Debian system.

Making Space for the Debian System

Having decided how much space you can devote to the Debian system, the first step is to make room on a disk for your Linux partitions. In the ideal case of having a machine you can use exclusively for running Linux, you can skip this section entirely and begin the installation process. When the time comes to create Linux partitions, just delete any existing partitions in cfdisk.

Another simple case occurs when you already have a partitioned drive. Some PCs are supplied with the disk partitioned into two, which usually appear as C: and D: drives under Windows. If this is the case, and you think that the D: partition is about the right size for your Debian system, you can simply copy any files you want to keep to the C: partition, and then start the installation. You will be able to delete the second DOS partition from cfdisk, and then use the space to create whatever Linux partitions you require.

Difficulties begin when there is just a single DOS or Windows partition, and you want to convert this partition into a dual boot Windows and Debian machine. In this case, the most common solution is to totally reformat the hard disk, putting a new Windows installation in a smaller partition to leave space for Linux. This inevitably means a certain amount of work—exactly how much depends on your circumstances.

If you have only a few important files, it may be that backing these up and reinstating them afterward is the best bet. If, on the other hand, you have a large amount of data and no high-capacity backup device, you might want to look at the non-destructive partitioning technologies. If the data has any value, you should still have it backed up, but at least you should not need to restore all the files, and repeat any customization you've carried out on your Windows installation.

After repartitioning a machine, there is some debate over whether Linux or Windows should be installed first. In practice, either should work fine. But if in doubt, the author's personal preference is to install Windows first. If you install another operating system on a machine that is already running Linux, you may have to boot Linux from a rescue disk and re-install the Linux Loader program before you can boot Linux normally again.

There is also a question of how to partition the disk before beginning the installation. If Windows is installed, you can run the fdisk program (which is a little like the Linux cfdisk program, described here, but more limited) to delete your current DOS partition and create a new, smaller one. Alternatively, you can boot from a Debian rescue disk, begin the installation process, and run the Linux cfdisk. If you do this, but still want to install Windows before Debian, you can safely reboot after partitioning the disk, install Windows, and then re-run the Debian installer and complete the process at a later date.

FIPS

One alternative to reformatting, at least for users with FAT16 partitions, is FIPS (the First nondestructive Interactive Partition Splitting program). This is a simple partition-splitting utility supplied under the GPL. Once existing data on your C: disk has been compacted (using a tool supplied with Windows), just run FIPS and it will convert your single primary DOS partition into two. You can then delete the second one and use the space to create Linux partitions.

The main limitation is that it is an old program, and doesn't know anything about the new FAT32 disk format, so many Windows 98 users will lose out. Nevertheless, if you do have a FAT16-based system, it is a simple and effective way of repartitioning without reformatting. If you think it fits the bill, download it from http://bmrc. berkeley.edu/people/chaffee/fips/fips.html.

PartitionMagic

PartitionMagic is a commercial solution to the problem of partition management. It is a graphical tool that allows, not only creation and deletion of complete partitions, but also moving and resizing operations (see Figure 3.3). Recent versions are aware of all kinds of Windows partitions, as well as Linux ext2 partitions, and several other types.

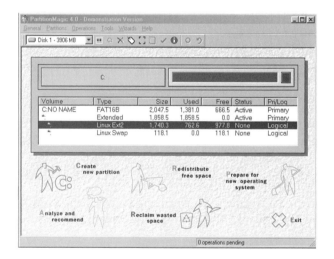

Figure 3.3

PartitionMagic may be the easiest answer if you have complex partitioning problems.

For the first-time Linux user, the main benefit of this program is that it provides an easy way to shrink your existing Windows partitions, even in cases where FIPS won't work. It can also resize ext2 partitions, in case you ever want to rearrange an existing Linux installation. And since PartitionMagic can create new Linux partitions, you may want to use it to complete your partition set up, and skip the partitioning stage on the standard installation entirely.

If you want to try this program, look at the supplier's Web site:

http://www.powerquest.com/

Creating New Partitions

There are several methods of creating Linux partitions. If you have used the PartitionMagic program to resize a DOS partition, you can simply go on and create one or more Linux ext2 partitions, plus a Linux swap partition, and then ignore the partitioning stage in the normal Debian installation process. But most Debian users will use the Linux-based partitioning tool, cfdisk. You will get a chance to launch this program during the normal installation procedure, as described in Chapter 4. It is also possible to run the tool at any time while running Linux—simply log on as the root user and type **cfdisk** at the command prompt.

NOTE

There is another Linux disk-partitioning tool, confusingly called fdisk. This is also supplied with Debian, and it is the default partitioning tool used by some other Linux distributions. For typical users, it provides essentially the same functionality as cfdisk, but presents a less friendly user interface.

Using cfdisk

Many new users find manipulating a partition table a worrisome prospect. The cfdisk main screen should really carry a message that says "don't panic." When you add or delete partitions, you are really altering a temporary copy of the partition table. These edits are committed back to disk only when you select the Write option. If you make a mistake, just choose Quit and start again.

When you first start cfdisk, you will see a screen similar to the one shown in Figure 3.4. This screen shows the initial state of the partition table of a machine supplied with two DOS partitions (drives C: and D: under Windows). Use the up and down arrow keys to select which partition you are working on, and use the left and right arrows to select options from the menu at the bottom of the screen. Note that the size of each partition is initially shown in megabytes. Select the *Units* option (or just press **u**) if you want to see how many cylinders each partition is using. This option is useful if you need to determine whether your root partition lies below the 1024 cylinder boundary.

If there isn't already some unused space (in the sense of not already being part of a formatted partition) on the disk, the first step is to delete one of the existing partitions. In Figure 3.5, the partition hda5 (the D: drive under Windows) has been deleted. Be sure that any data you want to keep has been moved elsewhere before you do this.

Once part of the disk has been freed, you can start creating Linux partitions (see Figure 3.6). The *New* menu option will ask you whether you want to create a physical or logical partition—remember that you can only create four physical partitions, or three physical partitions plus some logical partitions. It will then prompt for the size of the new partition. When you create a partition, you will normally enter the size in megabytes. But, in order to maximize disk performance, the program rounds this size to the nearest whole number of cylinders. Don't worry if the actual size of the new partition is slightly different than the size you entered.

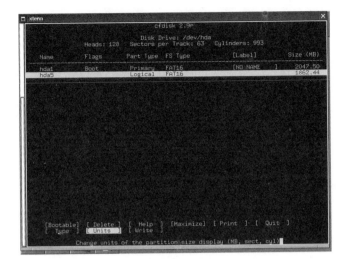

Figure 3.4

cfdisk provides a menu-based interface for partitioning your hard disk.

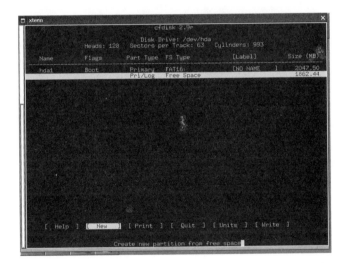

Figure 3.5

There is now a block of unused space at the end of the disk that's available for a Debian installation.

NOTE

The `cfdisk` user interface hides the fact that any logical partitions on a disk are contained within an extended partition. If an extended partition is needed, it will be created automatically. But since only one extended partition is allowed, this means that all the logical partitions on a disk must form one continuous block. This isn't normally a serious limitation.

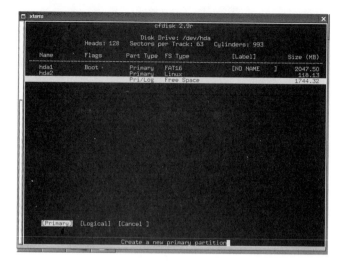

Figure 3.6

Creating new Linux partitions.

Each partition in the table has a code that specifies what kind of file system is to be stored on it. Newly created partitions have their code set correctly for a standard Linux ext2-format data partition. When you create the swap partition, you need to use the *Type* menu option in cfdisk to mark it as such (see Figure 3.7).

This same option can also be used to create partitions for use with other operating systems—you can, for instance, create a FAT partition that will become a D: drive under DOS. Note, however, that cfdisk just creates partitions without formatting them. Having created a FAT partition, you will need to format it under Windows using a command such as

```
format D:
```

The same is true if you ever create a new Linux partition and want to add it to an existing installation. (The installer automatically formats any partitions you are using.) But in this case, you need to use a Linux disk formatting program, such as

```
mke2fs /dev/hda5
```

A final concern are the *bootable* flags that can be set on each partition. These are really only a concern to expert users. If you have a partition from which DOS or Windows is booting, that partition should have the bootable flag set. It is safe to leave the flag off for all other partitions—even your Linux root partition.

Once you are happy with your new partition table, choose the Write option to save the changes you have made (see Figure 3.8). This is the only part of the whole process that actually writes to your hard disk, so check the table carefully before you confirm this operation!

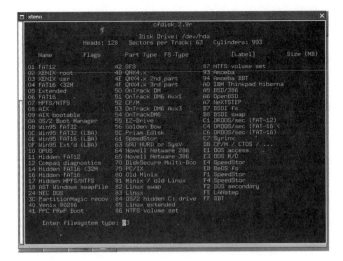

Figure 3.7

Changing the type of a newly created partition.

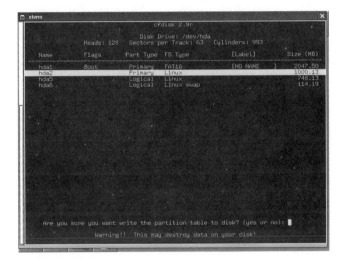

Figure 3.8

*The finished article contains two main Linux partitions (which will become root and /home partitions, respectively) and a swap partition. You must manually type **yes** to confirm the Write operation.*

Summary

By the time you have finished this chapter, you should have created a free area on your hard disk, ready to hold your new Debian installation. You should also have worked out a scheme for dividing this space up into partitions. If you want to get a simple home system up and running quickly, one large Linux partition plus a small swap partition will normally be the easiest option. But consider creating separate /home and /usr partitions: These will make your data safer, at the expense of a little extra complexity. For server installations, more complex partitioning arrangements might be appropriate, but it's best to experiment on a simple system first. If you have never partitioned a hard disk before, you might want to draw out your own diagram similar to Figure 3.1, and use this as a reference.

With some spare disk space ready, and your chosen partitioning scheme to hand, you are now ready to get out your Debian CDs and begin the installation.

CHAPTER 4

A Basic Installation

Having read about Debian's disk space and partitioning requirements, you can now look at the initial stages of Linux installation. Although there are a number of options for expert users, most people installing for the first time can accept the default values, and thus get a basic Debian workstation up and running very quickly.

Before you start, be sure that your hard disk is backed up, and that free disk partitions are ready for your installation. If you are using a tool such as PartitionMagic, or you have installed Linux on the machine before, you may already have created some Linux partitions. If not, simply make sure that there is either some unpartitioned space on the drive, or you have an empty partition that can be deleted. Once the installer has started, you will have a chance to run cfdisk in order to create any new Linux partitions you require.

Installation Media

The vast majority of users will be installing most of the Debian packages off a CD-ROM distribution, such as the set included with this book. If you want a more recent version, new Debian CDs are easy to obtain. If you are having trouble finding a local supplier, look at the Debian Web site at http://www. debian.org/

It is, however, possible to install from other media. If there is no way you can attach a Linux-compatible CD-ROM drive to the machine, it is theoretically possible to install all the packages from a copy of the distribution on a hard disk partition (either Linux or FAT format). More interestingly, it is also possible to install all but the basic parts of the distribution directly over a network connection.

At the moment, the availability of high-bandwidth connections means that a complete installation over the Internet is probably not an option for the majority of normal users, but this could change in the future. Large organizations that rely on Debian extensively might choose to keep an up-to-date mirror of the distribution on an internal server.

If you *do* have high-bandwidth Internet access and want to do a network installation, you should first find a nearby mirror of the main distribution site. This should speed up the downloading process, and help to spread the load of accesses away from the main site. There is a list of officially recognized mirrors (guaranteed to stay up to date and follow the standard archive structure) linked from the Debian home page.

Debian for Other Architectures

Debian has been ported to a number of architectures—there are some notes on this point in Chapter 2, "Getting Ready—Hardware." But getting CDs for non-Intel architectures may be a little more difficult. If you have a reasonably fast Internet connection, or know someone who does, you may find it easier to download the packages and make your own Debian CDs. Alternatively, simply install a base system and then configure dselect to grab the rest of the packages directly over the network.

The Debian installation program is essentially the same on all supported architectures (making slight allowances for differences in the hardware). The main difference you'll notice when carrying out a non-Intel installation is the method for initially booting the kernel—this method differs from architecture to architecture and is documented in text files supplied with the boot images for each supported platform.

The First Boot

The main Debian installation program runs under Linux. Thus, the first stage of the installation involves running a minimal Linux system, specifically designed to support the installer. The minimal system is usually called the *rescue* system, since it can also be used by experienced users to repair a damaged system. For most people with modern PCs, it is easiest to boot directly from a standard Debian CD-ROM.

All recent BIOSes allow the system to boot from an ATAPI (IDE) CD-ROM drive instead of the more normal choices of hard disk or floppy drive. CD booting may be disabled by default though, so don't worry if it doesn't work the first time. To try a CD-ROM boot, simply insert Debian CD 1 into your drive (if you have multiple drives, try the one with the lowest drive letter under Windows) and reboot the machine. If all goes well, you will see the Debian rescue disk boot screen, as shown in Figure 4.1.

If the boot process ignores your CD-ROM drive and boots from the hard disk as normal, reboot the machine again and enter the BIOS setup utilities (normally reached by pressing Delete just after the memory check stage of the boot process). The details of these utilities vary from machine to machine, but there will be some kind of menu-driven interface. The preferred boot device setting is generally found in the BIOS Features section. You will want to choose a option such as CDROM,C, meaning check the CD-ROM drive first, but if it is not possible to boot from that, use the first hard disk instead.

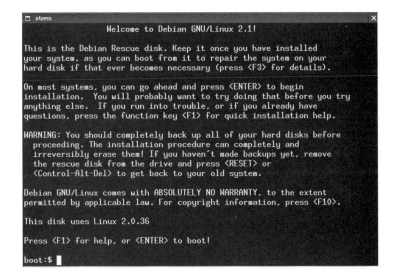

Figure 4.1

This screen shows a simple loading shell that allows you to start the real Debian rescue and install systems.

Once you have completed the installation, you may want to change this back to some other value—probably just C to boot from hard disk every time and ignore all other devices. Having reconfigured the BIOS, reboot once more so that the CD-ROM will be recognized.

Booting from Floppies

Occasionally, booting from a standard Debian CD-ROM is impossible, either because you are using a computer that doesn't support the process, or because you don't have an up-to-date Debian CD. In either case, you can use the more traditional method of booting the system from a floppy disk. Note that even if your BIOS does not allow you to boot from a CD-ROM, as long as the drive is recognized by the Linux kernel, you can still install the rest of the Debian packages off the CDs.

A typical Debian distribution includes a number of disk images. For an Intel system, you normally find these in the following directory:

```
dists/stable/main/disks-i386/current
```

This is relative to the root of a standard Debian CD-ROM, or the top level of a typical Debian FTP archive on the Internet.

There are separate images for 1.44MB and 1.2MB floppies—modern 3.5" drives always use the 1.44MB format. You will always need a rescue disk (such as resc1440.bin), and you will probably also want a drivers disk (such as drv1440.bin). If in doubt, make the drivers disk now—it takes only a few minutes.

Having selected the disk images you need, they must be written to newly formatted DOS floppy disks. This does NOT mean simply copying the file onto the disk as normal. The image files contain complete copies of live filesystems that must be written directly onto the disk surface. There are several methods for doing this. Under DOS or Windows, you can use the `rawrite2` program (from the tools directory of the CD). Just run the `rawrite2` program and it will prompt you for the image file to write and the disk drive to use.

It is also possible to write disk images under an existing UNIX system using the standard `dd` command. With a typical GNU/Linux installation, you can use something like

```
dd if=resc1440.bin of=/dev/fd0 && sync
```

On other UNIX systems, the name of the floppy disk device may be different.

Once you are happy with your boot disks, simply insert the rescue disk into drive A:, reset, and you should see the boot screen shown in Figure 4.1. If you do not, enter the BIOS setup utilities as described previously and make sure your machine hasn't been set up to ignore the floppy drive while booting.

Linux Start-Up

At the bottom of the rescue disk main screen, there is a `boot:` prompt. If you are rescuing an existing installation or booting on unusual hardware you may want to type extra options here, but for now, just press Return. First some data will be loaded, and then the Linux kernel itself will be loaded.

As the kernel starts, there will be a flurry of messages, mostly relating to the detection of various pieces of hardware in your system (see Figure 4.2). It's possible that a few of these may be errors, usually as a result of the kernel's attempts to find hardware that you don't have, but so long as the boot process completes successfully, don't worry about these for now. If you need to see any of the information displayed here, you can always look at it again by pressing <AltxF4>.

As soon as the kernel has finished booting for the first time, it will run the installer program itself, sometimes called `dbootstrap`. This is a semi-graphical program. It does not run in a normal GUI environment as such, but it presents a user interface based on simple character-based windows and menus. The sequence of steps in a standard installation is summarized in Figure 4.3.

Unless you are performing a very unusual installation, the first question will be whether to use color or monochrome screen displays (see Figure 4.4). Color makes some of the screens a little easier to follow. You will then see a release note from the particular rescue disk image you used. Continuing from this brings you to the main installer menu.

Occasionally, the kernel won't boot correctly—the system may hang or give an error message, either before or during kernel startup, or the machine may simply reboot silently. If one of these things happens, there is usually a simple solution; it is often just a matter of booting from an alternate disk. The section entitled "Installation Troubleshooting" at the end of this chapter describes a number of the more common problems.

```
xterm
Probing PCI hardware.
Calibrating delay loop.. ok - 233.47 BogoMIPS
Memory: 94852k/98304k available (1136k kernel code, 384k reserved, 1932k data)
Swansea University Computer Society NET3.035 for Linux 2.0
NET3: Unix domain sockets 0.13 for Linux NET3.035.
Swansea University Computer Society TCP/IP for NET3.034
IP Protocols: IGMP, ICMP, UDP, TCP
VFS: Diskquotas version dquot_5.6.0 initialized
Checking 386/387 coupling... Ok, fpu using exception 16 error reporting.
Checking 'hlt' instruction... Ok.
Linux version 2.0.36 (root@gondor) (gcc version 2.7.2.3) #2 Sun Feb 21 15:55:27
EST 1999
Starting kswapd v 1.4.2.2
Real Time Clock Driver v1.09
tpqic02: Runtime config, $Revision: 0.4.1.5 $, $Date: 1994/10/29 02:46:13 $
tpqic02: DMA buffers: 20 blocks, at address 0x282600 (0x28254c)
Ramdisk driver initialized : 16 ramdisks of 4096K size
loop: registered device at major 7
ide: i82371 PIIX (Triton) on PCI bus 0 function 57
    ide0: BM-DMA at 0xf000-0xf007
    ide1: BM-DMA at 0xf008-0xf00f
hda: ST36531A, 6204MB w/128kB Cache, CHS=790/255/63, UDMA
hdc: LTN242, ATAPI CDROM drive
ide0 at 0x1f0-0x1f7,0x3f6 on irq 14
ide1 at 0x170-0x177,0x376 on irq 15
Floppy drive(s): fd0 is 1.44M
FDC 0 is a post-1991 82077
:
```

Figure 4.2

A typical screen of boot messages, as displayed by the Linux kernel when it first starts up.

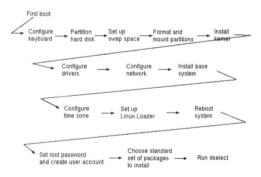

Figure 4.3

The main steps in a standard Debian installation.

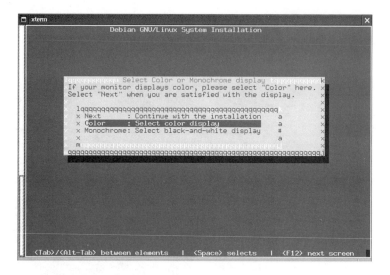

Figure 4.4

The first dbootstrap screen, and your initial contact with Linux applications.

Filling in the Installation Data

The remainder of the screens in the basic installation process revolves around telling dbootstrap where to find the main package archives (which is easy if you're installing from standard CD-ROMs), and setting up some fundamental parts of the system configuration.

The main installation menu is shown in Figure 4.5. For a typical installation, you will normally just follow the standard sequence of screens by constantly selecting the Next option, but it's always possible to skip back to an earlier screen if you realize that you've made a mistake.

EXTRA SCREENS FROM THE INSTALLER

Linux systems can provide multiple screen displays, called virtual consoles. You can switch between these by pressing Alt and a function key. In normal operation, these are used to allow you to run several login sessions, and switch quickly between them. When the Debian installer starts up, it actually runs on four of these virtual consoles. The main installation process, described here, appears on console 1 (Alt+F1). Console 2 can run a standard UNIX shell (albeit with a rather limited subset of commands available) and is provided mainly for the benefit of expert users.

Consoles 3 and 4 are used to display extra messages from the install program and the Linux kernel, respectively. If all goes well, you should never need to look at these screens. But if there is any problem during the installation, messages displayed here can give big clues as to what went wrong. In particular, if you are going to ask existing Linux users for advice on a specific problem, it's worth writing down the exact wording of any relevant messages.

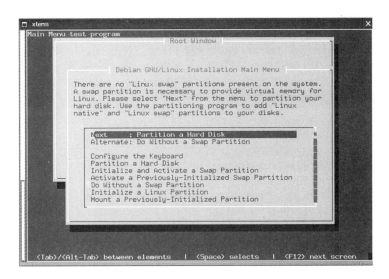

Figure 4.5

The installer main menu. Note that windows and menus within the installation system can sometimes scroll—the # characters represent a scroll bar.

The first real choice you'll need to make is which keyboard mapping to use. At this stage, this isn't hugely important—you'll be able to reconfigure it later if needed—but try choosing the option that best suits your system.

Generally, the next option is to partition your hard disk. If you have multiple hard disks, the installer prompts you to choose which disk to partition (normally the answer will be /dev/hda, the first IDE drive), and then runs the cfdisk program. At a minimum, you need to create one Linux native and one Linux swap partition, although you may want more. Partitioning schemes and the use of the cfdisk program are discussed in Chapter 3, "Getting Ready—Disk Space." Once you are happy with the arrangement of partitions, write the partition table, and then quit the program. You will be returned to the next screen in the main installation sequence.

The installer has a certain amount of built-in logic and if it detects that Linux partitions already exist, it will skip the partitioning stage. Needless to say, if you *do* want to run cfdisk, perhaps to replace the partitions you used for an old Linux installation with a new scheme, you can override the program's decision by explicitly selecting the Partition a hard disk option from the main menu.

Once the installer is satisfied that you have created Linux partitions, it prompts you to activate a partition to be used for swap space. If there is more than one valid swap partition on the disk, you are offered a choice of which one should be activated now. It is possible to use more than one swap partition, but second and subsequent ones must be configured manually later.

There are two options for activating a swap partition: with or without an initialization step. This is analogous to formatting a normal data partition. Swap partitions *must* be initialized before they can be used for the first time, and there is no harm in re-initializing a partition that has been used before, so the answer here will almost always be **yes**. Having chosen to initialize a partition, you are asked whether to check the disk surface for bad blocks. This takes a few moments, but could save you trouble later, so once again choose **yes**.

Next, you can format some Linux partitions and specify how they are to be used for the installation. At a minimum, you need to format and mount a root partition before any installation can take place. If you want a separate /usr partition, now is the time to set that up, too.

When you choose the Initialize Linux partition option, you will once again have the option to check the partition for bad blocks. For a large partition this can take some time, but it's worth performing the check, especially if you've never used the disk space before. The installer displays some messages while the formatting is taking place— these messages just give details of the exact arrangement of file catalog data on the disk surface. They are likely to be relevant only to system administrators trying to optimize the performance of large server-class systems.

When you initialize the first partition, the installer prompts you as to whether you want to make it the root partition. Mounting a root partition is vital before the installation can proceed any further, so the answer to this will almost certainly be **yes**. If you want any other partitions for use in your Debian installation (/usr, and perhaps /home and /usr/local), you can repeat the Initialize partition option. Now that you have a root partition set up, you can type in the name of the directory you want to use as the mount point for that partition. All file systems that you initialize from the installer will be automatically mounted whenever your new Debian system boots.

A second option allows you to mount previously initialized partitions, without losing any data stored on them. You could, for instance, use this to re-mount the /home partition from some previous Linux installation. Note that if you do this, you must either be sure to create new accounts for each user on the machine that has the same numeric user IDs as the accounts on the old system, or manually reset the owner IDs of all files on the partition to match the account setup of your new installation.

Managing UNIX user accounts is a complex subject in its own right, although fortunately many of the details are less important when there is only a small number of accounts on one machine. Some common techniques for managing user accounts are described in Chapter 6, "The First Steps in Debian."

Kernel Installation

Having mounted all the partitions you are planning to use, you finally get the chance to begin installing Debian files on the hard disk. First you install the Linux kernel itself, plus a selection of kernel modules. (These are generally drivers for more obscure pieces of hardware and are loaded when they are needed rather than being a permanent part of the kernel.)

If you have mounted more than one partition, you are shown a complete list of partitions and their mount points. Once you have accepted this list, the installer displays a list of media from which the kernel can be installed (see Figure 4.6). In virtually all cases, the answer will be whichever device (CD-ROM or floppy) you used to initially boot the rescue system. If this was a floppy, the installer automatically reads the required files with no additional information. Once files have been copied from the rescue floppy, you are prompted for a drivers floppy.

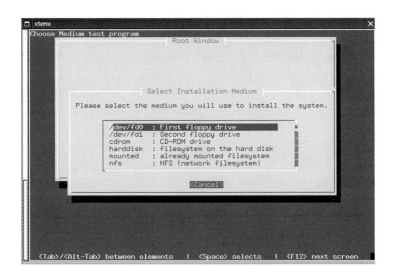

Figure 4.6
You can select the medium from which to install the Linux kernel.

If you are booting from a CD-ROM, however, you need to help it a little. First, you need to specify the Linux name of your CD-ROM device. If in doubt, for a standard IDE CD-ROM, first try /dev/hdc, and then try /dev/hdb. For SCSI devices, try /dev/scd0. Next, you are asked where the Debian archive is on the CD. (The default value, /debian, should be fine for any standard Debian CD you find.) Now, select the list option. This causes the installer to search the disk you have specified for directories appearing to contain the Debian rescue and driver images. On a normal CD, there will almost certainly be only one of these directories, but if the CD *does* contain multiple sets of disks with different version numbers, you'll normally want the set with the highest number.

Initial Configuration of the Kernel

Once the kernel is installed, you can perform additional configuration processes before the basic support files are copied on to the hard disk. First, you can configure the various loadable kernel modules that you have just installed. If you've had prior Linux experience, you might want to quickly check through all the categories at this stage, but for a first-time installer on a standard machine, most of these categories are unlikely to be important. If you want to install the main Debian packages from a non-standard CD-ROM (modern ATAPI devices work without any intervention), check the cdrom section for a module to control your particular card.

If your machine has a network card, you also have the chance to configure it at this stage. Obviously, this is particularly important if you are planning to install Debian packages over the network, but it's worth configuring it now anyway. Open the net section and look for a module that suits your card.

When you load certain driver modules, you can pass various parameters to help the module detect the hardware it is supposed to control. For modern PCI devices, extra parameters are likely unnecessary, but some ISA cards cannot be reliably detected unless you tell the driver which system resources the card has been configured to use (see Chapter 2 for a discussion of the ISA bus and its shortcomings). A typical command line to specify shared memory and interrupt numbers might look something like this:

```
io=0x220 irq=7
```

Getting Connected

During installation, you have the option to set up a network connection for the machine. This applies only to permanent connections (normally via Ethernet). If you are going to use a dial-up network connection only, this is configured later using a separate program (see Chapter 8, "Advanced Configuration"). If you *do* have any form of network connection (other than to a private network that you run yourself), now is the time to ask your network administrator for your IP address plus any other details of the network you are using.

There is one piece of network configuration that everyone should do—specify the hostname of the computer. Machines connected to the Internet have multi-part names, for instance, adzel.solar-spice.com. In this case, adzel is the local hostname. If you have a permanent Internet connection, your network administrator will probably give you a hostname for the machine. If not, you might be able to ask for a name of your choice. But Debian systems (like any modern UNIX) always need to have a hostname set, even if there is no Internet connection.

If you have even a small private network, giving each machine a memorable name is vital to avoiding confusion. If your machine is running as a standalone system, the name you enter isn't really important. In any case, you now have an excuse to give your computer a silly name!

Once you have entered a suitable hostname, the installer asks you whether you want to configure a permanent network connection. If so, you are asked to enter additional information. The first piece of information is the name of the Internet domain in which your machine is named. For a computer named `adzel.solar-spice.com`, the domain name is `solar-spice.com`.

Next comes the machine's IP address, a value consisting of four numbers separated by periods. IP addresses uniquely identify every machine connected to the Internet (or any private network that uses Internet-like technology).

NOTE

Note that in the near future, some networks may begin switching to a new generation of networking technology called IPv6, which uses longer addresses. Basic IPv6 support is included in new Linux kernels, and future versions of Debian will offer options to use IPv6 addressing. If your network is using IPv6, the administrator should tell you this and help you set up your connection.

You are also asked for `netmask` and `broadcast` values. If you haven't been told these, the installer guesses defaults, which are correct for most conventional network installations. The final essential parameter—which only normally applies to networks forming part of the Internet—is the gateway address. This is the IP address of a machine (either a dedicated router or, for small sites, a specially set up computer) that controls the flow of traffic between networks.

If you have an Internet connection, you also want to set up a method for the computer to connect to the Internet Domain Name Service (DNS), the system that translates between hostnames and IP addresses. If your network administrator has given you the address of a DNS server, you should use that.

If there is no DNS server on your local network, you can tell the installer that the machine should act as its own DNS server. This option does not rely on any other machine, but you must be sure that the `bind` package is installed when you reach the package-selection stage (see Chapter 5, "Making Your Selection").

Finally, after confirming the details for your network connection, you are asked which device represents the primary network interface. For most users, this is `eth0`, the first Ethernet adapter detected in the machine. Note that the common UNIX abstraction of making hardware devices appear as special files in the `/dev` directory does not extend to network adapters.

There is a separate option here for users of PC Card network adapters. The configuration details for these are stored in a slightly different manner, thus reflecting the fact that these devices can be inserted and removed while the computer is running.

Once you have set up your network configuration in the installer, there is a good chance that you will never need to touch it again. But if the network details ever *do* change, you will want to look at the `/etc/init.d/network` configuration file.

SETTING UP A SIMPLE PRIVATE NETWORK

Many people now own more than one computer, and setting up a private Ethernet to connect all the machines in your house can make transferring files and sharing resources, such as printers, much easier. With a little more work (unfortunately beyond the scope of this book), a Debian system can even act as a fully functional network gateway by sharing a single dial-up Internet connection between all the computers on the network. Many computer shops now sell all the components required to set up a small network and offer advice on subjects such as cabling and hubs.

Machines attached to small private networks are normally given IP addresses in the form 192.168.1.xxx, where xxx is a number between 1 and 254. Obviously, each machine on the network should have a unique address. If you are using addresses of this form, the correct netmask is 255.255.255.0, and you will initially want to set it to an Internet gateway machine.

In practice, you will normally refer to each computer on the network by name. For small networks, it is normally not worth the hassle of using the complete Internet Domain Name System for mapping between names and addresses. Instead, edit the standard UNIX configuration file /etc/hosts to list the names for your local network, as described in Chapter 10, "Exploring the X Window System."

The Base System Installation

By this point, you have provided enough configuration information to allow installation of the core GNU/Linux tools, which make up the Debian base system. If you are installing from a CD-ROM, the base system file is located in exactly the same way as the kernel—in fact, it will normally be stored in the same location. The complete base system image will have a name like base2_1.tgz (for a Debian 2.1 system).

For machines with no CD-ROM drive or network connection, it is possible to install the base system from a pile of floppy disks. This is a more awkward option—as of version 2.1, the base system occupies seven 1.44MB images, each of which must be written to a disk and then inserted in turn at the appropriate moment.

One final option, which some people might find useful, is to install the base system from a hard disk partition. This can be either a normal Linux partition or a DOS partition. If you want to do this, copy the base2_1.tgz file (or the equivalent file from a newer Debian version) to a partition that isn't going to be reformatted during the installation. When you reach the base system installation stage, you have the chance to mount this partition and then locate the base system archive in the same way you do when installing from a CD-ROM.

With the base system installed, there is one final question to answer: which UNIX time zone configuration file to use. Choose the file for the nearest city available. You also are asked whether the system's clock is set to GMT (coordinated universal time) or to local time. Common practice in the UNIX world is to leave the main system clock set to GMT. As long as you have set the time zone correctly, programs attempting to read the local time will still get the correct answer. But Windows always expects the clock to be set to local time, so if you are expecting to use Windows enough to be bothered that the time is wrong, select local time instead.

If you want to change the setting of the system clock while running Linux, use commands such as

```
hwclock —set —date="16:14:45"
hwclock —hwtosys
```

Preparing to Reboot

With a minimal Linux system installed, you must now install LILO, the LInux LOader. This is a tiny program run by the BIOS which loads the Linux kernel. Later, you can configure LILO to boot your existing Windows installation instead of booting Linux. (For details on reconfiguring LILO, see the sidebar entitled "Configuring the Linux Loader.")

For now, simply select the Make bootable option from the installer, and answer **yes** when asked whether to install a boot block and whether to make Linux boot as the default operating system. If your Debian root partition is a logical partition (as described in Chapter 3), you are asked which primary partition you want to use for the boot loader—the default should always be correct.

You also have the chance to create a boot floppy disk at this point. This is a little like the rescue disk, but it does not contain the dbootstrap program. Instead, it simply boots a Linux kernel and then mounts your normal root partition, just as if you were booting from hard disk. If you are performing a straightforward installation, it usually won't hurt to skip this step. But it *can* get you out of trouble if, for any reason, it becomes impossible to boot your Debian installation. A typical use for a boot floppy would be to boot Linux for the first time after installing a new operating system, such as Windows, which normally overwrites the Linux boot loader system. If you want a boot floppy, simply insert a blank disk when prompted: The installer will format it and add the Linux kernel.

After You Reboot

When you select reboot, the machine will go through its normal startup checks, and then, instead of loading Windows, you will see the LILO prompt. If you wait for a few moments, LILO will automatically load the Linux kernel from the hard disk.

You should see a set of boot messages similar to those from the first boot. But when this is complete, you see some extra startup messages, produced by the init system. This is the suite of programs and scripts responsible for performing system setup tasks like mounting filesystems and starting up the network subsystem. Once your system is fully installed, init scripts are also responsible for starting any programs such as Web servers that need to be running all the time.

Once the Debian system has started up, you have a few more setup jobs. The first is to set the password of the *root* account. This root account is a special user account that has privileged access to the system. You will use it for installing new software, editing system-wide configuration options, and managing other user accounts. In theory, you can use the root account for all your computing but, by doing so, you are bypassing all the security and safety checks that UNIX-like systems normally provide. Experienced system administrators will go out of their way to avoid logging in as root unless it is absolutely necessary.

In recognition of this, the Debian installation system automatically offers you the chance to create a normal (unprivileged) user account as well. This is what you should use for day-to-day work. Debian, like any UNIX system, can provide many user accounts and the UNIX security model allows each user to keep personal files private. Instructions for creating more new accounts, and for managing the accounts on your system, can be found in Chapter 6.

The basic installation process is now complete, and all that remains is to use the dselect program (described fully in Chapter 5) to install the final complement of packages that will make up your complete installation.

Debian has what is generally considered to be a fine-grained package management system—you can choose exactly what is installed on your system, but at the expense of having to look through a rather long list of packages to find exactly what you want. As of Debian version 2.1, the installer gives you the option of pre-setting the package manager with a number of different package selections (see Figure 4.7). Note that these packages aren't installed immediately. But if you choose one of the options here, the dselect program will be started with the chosen package selection set up. You just need to set up the dselect access method, and then run the Update and Install options.

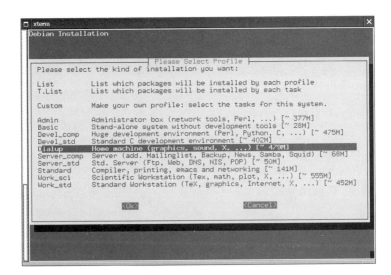

Figure 4.7

You can choose from a variety of default installation profiles.

Don't worry too much about the exact choice of packages you install—you can run dselect whenever you want to add and remove packages as you choose. The remaining chapters of this book talk about some of the more important and useful packages in the standard Debian distribution, but it is only possible to cover a tiny proportion of what is available. It's always worth browsing through the package listings yourself to get a feel for the wealth of software available with GNU/Linux systems.

CONFIGURING THE LINUX LOADER

On Intel systems, the Linux kernel is booted using a program called LILO. This program can be configured in a number of ways by editing the file /etc/lilo.conf using your favorite text editor. (If you are not familiar with UNIX editors, consult Chapter 7, "A Tour of the Packages.") You must then run the lilo command to commit the changes you have made. Since this is a critical system-management task, you must always be logged on using the root account to edit /etc/lilo.conf or run lilo.

The lilo.conf file contains one section of global options, followed by a section for each operating system that can be booted. Each operating system section begins with a line starting image= (to boot a Linux kernel) or other= (to boot some other operating system). A full list of options can be found by typing

man lilo.conf

If you are going to use your machine as a dual-boot Debian and Windows system, you should add the following lines at the beginning of the file:

prompt

timeout=100

This tells LILO that it should always prompt you to specify which operating system you want booted, but to boot the first operating system specified in the file if you do not reply within 10 seconds. (LILO measures time in tenths of a second.)

Now, to allow Windows to boot, you should add the following section to the end of the file:

```
other=/dev/hda1
        table=/dev/hda
        label=windows
```

This code assumes that Windows is installed on the first partition of the hard disk. It allows you to boot from this partition by typing **windows** at the LILO prompt. If you want Windows to be the default operating system, simply swap the Windows and Linux sections of the file around so that the Windows section comes first.

What's Next

Once you have completed your basic installation and familiarized yourself with the dselect program, you can begin setting up your Debian system in earnest. For most people, the first priority is to establish a graphical user interface. This, plus a number of other important setup tasks, is discussed in Chapter 6.

Alternatively, you can just log on straight away using the unprivileged account you created earlier and start familiarizing yourself with the command-line tools from the basic Debian system. Please don't use the root account for experimentation. Explaining the power of the UNIX command line would take up a good-sized book by itself. But if you have a little previous UNIX knowledge, do try experimenting—and remember the online UNIX manual. For instance, to view the options of the shutdown command, type

```
man shutdown
```

You can page through the documentation by pressing space, and leave the manual browser by pressing q or by using the standard UNIX interrupt keystroke, Control×C.

If your computer has an Internet connection via a local area network, you should already have that configured and working—you'll probably want to install packages such as Web browsers in order to take advantage of this. If you are using dial-up Internet access, a little more configuration is needed: This is discussed in Chapter 8.

Switching Off

Finally, at some point, you will want to shut the machine down. You should never switch off or reset a Linux-based system without shutting it down properly first. If you do not shut the system down properly, it will spend several minutes running consistency checks on your disk partitions the next time you switch it on. In the worst-case scenario, serious disk corruption could occur. The standard way to shut down is to log on using the root account and type

```
shutdown -h now
```

The -h stands for halt. You will see a list of messages as various operating systems components are disabled, and then finally the System halted message will appear, which indicates that it is safe to switch off. If you specify the -r option instead, the machine will reboot. On a standard Debian system it is also possible to safely reboot by pressing Ctrl×Alt×Delete. Finally, some graphical user interfaces provide their own methods for shutting down the system.

You may have noticed the now option passed to the shutdown command. As you might expect, this causes the system to start the shutdown process straight away. But if you are running a server machine that may have other users connected over the network, you can also use the shutdown command to schedule a system halt or reboot at some point in the future. To give users 15 minutes grace to finish their work and log off, try

```
shutdown -h +15
```

In this case, users will receive a series of warning messages as shutdown time approaches. Read the manual page for more details.

Installation Troubleshooting

By following the previous steps, you should be able to install a recent Debian release on virtually any modern PC (or, with slight modifications, many other architectures as well). Occasionally, problems may arise, usually while attempting to boot the Linux kernel.

If all else fails, consider contacting established Linux users. If you don't know anyone with Linux experience, contact a local Linux Users' Group, or ask questions on an Internet newsgroup or mailing list. There are some links to different areas of the Linux community in Chapter 11, "And Finally—Welcome to the Community."

Boot Parameters

Some older and more obscure pieces of hardware are difficult for an operating system kernel to correctly and safely detect. Some boot parameters that you can provide for the Linux kernel and that might be useful are documented on the help screens available by pressing function keys at the rescue disk boot screen. The most useful ones relate to detection of IDE devices. Some older machines cause problems when the kernel tries to identify the geometry of their hard disks. It is possible to specify this manually at the boot prompt. It is also possible to supply hints that specific IDE devices are ATAPI CD-ROM drives—although this shouldn't be necessary for any but the oldest devices.

Boot Image Problems

Some machines can run Debian, but do not agree with the standard boot images supplied as the bootable section on the Debian CD 1 and in the `resc1440.bin` file. The most common problem involves the format used to store the Linux kernel. There are two formats for the kernel: `zImage` and the newer `bzImage`, which is used on the standard boot images. Some machines, notably laptops, are unable to load `bzImage` kernels. A common symptom is a silent reboot of the machine immediately after loading the kernel.

If you think you are experiencing a kernel format error, Debian 2.1 includes an alternative rescue image (`resc1440-tecra.bin`, and also written as the bootable part of CD 2). The `tecra` in the name, incidentally, refers to the Toshiba Tecra series of laptops, but this fix applies to a number of other systems.

There are also *safe* variants of the rescue disk images. These variants use a different version of the Linux loader software that may be able to cope with bugs in certain BIOSes. If you are having trouble booting, especially on an old machine, it may be worth trying one of these disk images instead.

The Worst Case: Linux Won't Boot

Unfortunately, a few machines completely refuse to boot the Linux kernel and give errors such as `Invalid compressed format`.

This is rarely Linux's fault—more often it is an indication of a subtle hardware defect even if the machine apparently works fine under Windows. The most common cause of this problem is a substandard memory chip. Since the Linux kernel allocates system memory differently to Windows, it is possible for a memory problem that caused, at worst, an occasional error under Windows to prevent a Linux system from booting entirely.

Such problems are not always easy to diagnose: The memory check that the BIOS performs when the machine first starts up is not at all comprehensive and frequently misses subtle problems. Special memory-check programs can perform better, but even these do not exercise the RAM devices in the same way that a normal program does.

If you suspect a memory problem (or, for that matter, any other hardware fault), the best diagnosis is to physically trace the defective component. If your computer has more than one bank of memory, try removing each in turn to see whether that allows the machine to boot. Alternatively, if you have access to another computer that uses the same kind of memory, try swapping RAM modules between the two machines.

Summary

Having read this chapter, you should be familiar with the steps required to install the Linux kernel, and a few basic tools, on your machine. Once this is complete, the installer will automatically start the `dselect` package management program. Chapter 5 explains how you can use `dselect` to install software from the huge selection of packages supplied with the Debian distribution. With this step complete, you will be ready to start exploring Debian yourself.

CHAPTER 5

Making Your Selection

This chapter looks at the Debian package-management system, which is a set of programs that provide an easy method for installing new software on your GNU/Linux system. Behind the scenes, the package-management system is also keeping records of which packages you have installed, and which files on your system belong to which package. This makes it easy to remove a package that you decide you don't need, or upgrade it to the latest version.

What Is a Package?

Conceptually, a *package* is any unit of software that can be installed on your computer. Debian takes a fine-grained approach to package management. This means that you have a very high level of control over the software installed. But conversely, you may need to install a number of different packages to accomplish one task. An example is *The Gimp*, a complex image-manipulation program. As well as the core gimp package, there are optional packages that contain additional data files and the program's documentation.

In practice, a package is a bundle of files, rather like standard UNIX tar.gz archives, or the ZIP files common with DOS and Windows. But as well as containing the files that make up the program you want to install, a package file contains a number of other pieces of information. The most important extra details are

- The package version number. Comparing the version numbers of the most recent packages available with those already installed allows automatic upgrading of the system.
- A set of scripts (simple programs) that are run automatically when the package is installed or removed. This

allows the package to seamlessly configure itself and integrate into the system. These scripts can perform the functions of the installation wizards supplied with many Windows applications.

- A list of package dependencies. One Debian package can either require some other package, or declare a conflict that makes the two mutually exclusive.

There are also various other conventions followed by Debian packages, especially regarding placement of resource files on the system. These conventions are set out in the Debian policy and packaging manuals. From a user's perspective, the most important rule is that each package must create its ownsubdirectory of /usr/doc. Any important documentation files are found there.

Debian packages are supplied as files with a .deb extension. The main part of the name customarily has a standard format. Consider, for instance, the package file named freeciv_1.7.2-3.deb. The first part, freeciv, is the official Debian name of the package, and should always be lowercase. (Freeciv, incidentally, is a popular UNIX strategy game.) After the underscore comes the main version number, which signifies that the package was built from the 1.7.2 release of the standard Freeciv code. The final number, after a hyphen, is the Debian version number. This indicates that this is the third Debian package built from this version of the standard code, and indicates that there have been some minor modifications to the packaging process since the first package was built.

Installing from .deb packages is almost always the easiest way to add new software to your Debian system. But occasionally .deb files are not available. Various solutions for installing non-Debian software are discussed toward the end of this chapter.

Debian Archives

There are a number of methods for obtaining Debian software—CD-ROM and Internet FTP archives are the main distribution mechanisms, so those methods are considered here. Regardless of the method used for distributing the software, Debian archives have a well-defined structure. The top level of any archive is likely to contain a number of incidental files and directories, which contain information such as the Debian FAQ. They also contain a directory named dists. It is in the dists directory that all the main Debian software is stored. Some examples from a typical Debian FTP archive are shown in Figure 5.1.

Within the dists directory, there are sub-directories corresponding to various complete releases of the distribution. In the case of a CD-ROM, there is normally only one distribution: the stable release from the time the disk was made. But Internet archives often carry the latest unstable version too, and, if appropriate, a frozen distribution undergoing final testing and bug-fixing before it is marked as stable.

As well as specifying distributions by the unstable/frozen/stable classification, you can also refer to a specific version of Debian by its development code-name. Some Internet archives may include versions of the distribution earlier than the current stable version, and these can be accessed only by name. The code names of recent versions are shown in Table 5.1.

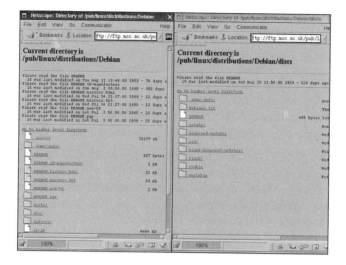

Figure 5.1

Views of the root and dists directories in a typical Debian archive site.

Table 5.1   Development of Code Names for Recent Debian Releases

Name	Debian Release
boo	1.3
hamm	2.0
slink	2.1
potato	Not yet stable, but expected to become release 2.2
sid	Experimental code for unsupported hardware architectures

And in case you didn't believe it, yes, they are all named after characters from the animated film *Toy Story*.

Sub-Distributions

The complete Debian distribution is split into several sub-distributions, each of which occupies its own directory hierarchy. Not surprisingly, it is the main section that contains the most important packages. The packages under this directory represent the Debian distribution itself—all these packages meet the requirements set out in the Debian policy manual. The base system, together with the majority of other packages that most users will want, is included in the main section.

Additional packages, which don't meet the policy guidelines but are nevertheless considered useful to Debian users, are found in the contrib and non-free directories. These aren't supported to the same level that the main packages are, but nonetheless they have all been specifically packaged for Debian and should install cleanly.

In the case of non-free packages, they are not free software as specified in the Debian Free Software guidelines (see Chapter 1, "Introducing Debian"). This doesn't necessarily mean that you have to pay to use them—most are free for non-commercial use, and many are free for commercial use too. But they may be covered by unacceptable restrictions, or the source code may not be available. If you want to use a package from the non-free section—especially if you want to use or distribute it commercially—you should look at the package documentation (in the directory /usr/doc/<packagename>) and check the license before doing so.

Within each sub-distribution directory, there is a structure of directories that is fairly self-explanatory. If you are using an Internet archive, you will see binary-<arch> directories for each supported architecture (on a CD-ROM there will normally be only one architecture). Within the architecture directories, the package files are divided according to their function into a number of groups. These are discussed in Chapter 7, "A Tour of the Packages."

NOTE

> There has been some debate about moving the contrib and non-free sections off the master FTP server and onto another location, in order to clarify the fact that these are distinct from the core distribution. At the time of writing, it is not clear whether this is going to happen. But if it does, there will be announcements on the Debian Web site. The main practical consequence of this split is that users who routinely download packages from the Internet may want to add the new server as an extra apt package source. The apt program and the concept of package sources are discussed in the section on Internet installation.

Joining the Arms Trade?

Some common pieces of software—generally those providing encryption services—are considered by the U.S. government to represent military technology. As a result, downloading programs such as the popular pgp e-mail privacy tool could make you a potential international arms smuggler! The Debian project has avoided this problem by making certain packages available only from the FTP service (which is located in Germany) at ftp://non-US.debian.org/debian-non-US.

plus various mirror sites, all outside of the United States. The non-U.S. distribution sites have the same structure as the main site, but contain only a few packages—tools such as pgp, and the ssh system for creating secure login connections to remote computers. If you are installing packages over the Internet, you can have the installer automatically merge the non-U.S. packages with the main list. But if you have installed the main distribution from CD and just want one or two non-U.S. packages, it may be easier to download them using a Web browser and then install them manually.

The Package-Management Programs

There are several layers to the package-management system. At the lowest levels are a set of library routines that will only be of interest to programmers seeking to replace parts of the package-management system. On top of this comes the dpkg program, a command-line tool that allows installation and removal of packages, plus many other operations. The dpkg tool is used mainly by expert users, but there is a brief description of one situation in which it can prove useful at the end of this chapter.

The package-management system has been evolving for some time, and it is still improving now. In recent versions of Debian, dpkg is accompanied by apt, a system that handles fetching of package files from multiple locations. The apt tools also automate the process of resolving the dependencies of each new package that you install. This is now the preferred way to perform Debian installations over the Internet, and it also simplifies the process of upgrading a Debian-based machine.

For many users, virtually all the package-management operations can be performed via the dselect program. This program provides a friendly, interactive front-end to the whole package-management system, and allows easy browsing of the available packages. The dselect program does not actually install packages itself. But it automatically runs the apt and dpkg tools in order to fetch and install the packages you have selected. The package-management system is summarized in Figure 5.2.

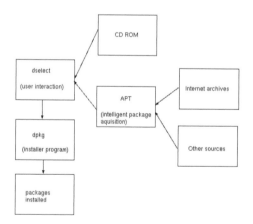

Figure 5.2

Structure of the Debian package-management system.

While dselect is the part of the package-management system most people will see, it is really a front-end layer on top of the other tools. Therefore, it is possible to replace it with some other user interface. The gnome-apt program, currently under development, should soon provide an alternative to dselect for users who prefer a windowed interface (see Figure 5.3). Although the two programs may look different, they provide the same basic set of features, and the principles of selecting and installing packages remain the same.

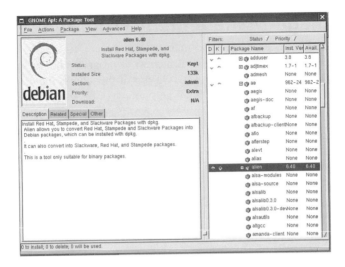

Figure 5.3

An early development version of gnome-apt—a new package management interface that's likely to gradually replace dselect for many purposes.

Starting the Package Manager

The dselect program runs automatically at the end of any Debian installation. It can also be run manually at any time—although you'll need to be logged on using the root account if you actually want to modify the system, rather than just browse the list of available packages. When dselect first starts, it displays a menu, which guides you through the main stages you'll use when updating your system (see Figure 5.4).

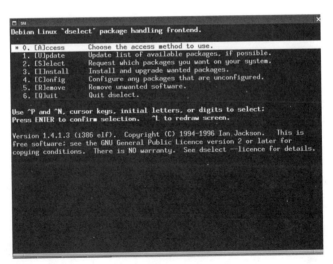

Figure 5.4

The dselect main menu, with entries corresponding to the main steps involved in updating your system.

Setting Up Your Package Sources

The first time you run `dselect`, you must tell the system where to find Debian packages. Thus, the Access option is the first item on the `dselect` main menu. There are a number of possible access methods to choose from (see Figure 5.5)—but as of Debian 2.1, many of these are obsolete. The two that are likely to be of interest are the `multi_cd` method (which you'll use to install from standard Debian CD sets) and `apt`, which is what you want if you are performing a network-based installation, or upgrading an existing distribution over the network.

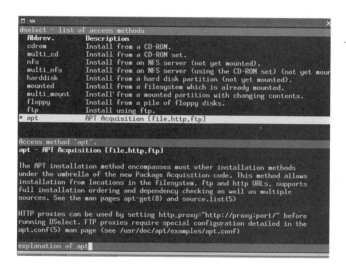

Figure 5.5

The package manager can use various methods for locating package files.

Actually, the `apt` system can also be used for installing packages from CD-ROM, so the `multi_cd` option will ultimately become obsolete, too. But at the moment, `dselect` doesn't allow you to easily configure a CD-ROM drive as an `apt` package source, so this option isn't recommended—yet. If you *do* want to try using the `apt` system with CD-ROM sets, read the manual page for the `apt-cdrom` package. Note that the `apt` system is gradually becoming more and more central to Debian package management, and in the future, it seems likely that `apt` will become the standard method for installing from CD-ROMs as well.

Installing from CD-ROM

Upon selecting the `multi_cd` access method, you are first prompted for the UNIX device name of your CD-ROM device. If you've already installed the Debian base system from a CD, the installer already created the new device name, `/dev/cdrom`, as a link to the real device you used then. You will almost certainly be able to accept the default here.

Generally, Debian is supplied on several CDs. The complete Debian CD set consists of four disks—two containing the actual packages, and two with source code. The disks supplied with this book correspond to the first two disks of the full set. Whenever you set up the `multi_cd` access method, you should always insert the *last* CD in the set that contains binary packages, since this CD contains information about the contents of previous CDs. Once you have provided this CD, the access method will search the CD for the various sub-distributions (main, contrib, non-free, and non-U.S.). Your CD set may not include some of these sub-distributions. If you are prompted for the location of a particular sub-distribution, you should normally just reply **none**.

Installing Over a Network

There are two access methods that allow `dselect` to obtain packages using the Internet file transfer protocol (FTP). But unless you are an expert user, you should ignore the `ftp` option, and use the new `apt` system instead. If you are doing a network installation for the first time, it is worth first locating your nearest archive site, and then familiarizing yourself with the directory structure using your favorite Web browser or FTP tool.

The `apt` system is based around the concept of a *source list*—a file that can specify any number of locations from which Debian packages can be obtained. For an initial installation, you will only need one entry in your source list, but you can add more later. The `apt` package fetcher automatically merges the lists of packages available from each source.

The first thing to configure is the root of the Debian archive site you are using. This is specified in URL format. Depending on which mirror site you are using, the Debian archive root will often be a sub-directory of an archive containing many other files. The Debian root directory will always contain the `dists` directory.

Next, you need to specify the *distribution tag* that you want to use—this refers to the sub-directory of the `dists` directory in the archive. For a first installation, you can almost always type **stable** here. Once you have gained some experience with Debian and you want to live dangerously, you might like to try the unstable distribution instead, but ignore that for now. If you prefer, you can also specify distribution versions by their code names, as listed in Table 5.1.

Finally, you are prompted for a list of sub-distributions to look for. In a standard archive, the default value of `main contrib non-free` will normally be correct, but you might like to add extra entries if you are using a non-standard site. You have now defined a complete entry for the source list.

When you have finished, you have the chance to add another site to the source list. If you need any encryption-related packages, add your nearest mirror of the non-U.S. archive—give the details for this in exactly the same way you did the main archive. If plans to move the `contrib` and `non-free` packages out of the main Debian archives and onto their own servers go ahead, you will probably also want to add an extra source list entry for these packages.

For reference, you might like to know that the `apt` source list is stored in the text file `/etc/apt/sources.list`. One line of this file corresponds to each package source. The format is quite complex, so it is best not to add new lines to this file yourself. However, you may find it useful to manually remove lines from this file when they are no longer required.

To check that the paths have been set up correctly, perform an Update operation. `dselect` should download a list of available packages from each site on your source list.

Updating and Installing Debian

With the package sources set up, you can now follow through the remaining stages on the `dselect` menu. The Update option causes the program to scan all the available package archives and fetch a list of packages that can be installed. If you are using a CD-ROM set, you need to perform this step only once—the first time you use the set. If, however, you are downloading packages from the Internet, updated package versions (usually fixes for security-related bugs) may appear from time to time, so it is worth performing regular updates so that `dselect` can automatically pick these up.

The next stage is normally to enter the package selection screens (described in the next section). But if there are already packages selected for installation, as there are if you chose one of the standard package selections from the installer, you can proceed directly to the installation stage.

When you select Install, `dselect` will first download any packages that are required from FTP archives. It will then begin uncompressing and configuring packages. Most packages install automatically. Others do need extra information, and run simple interactive configuration utilities during the installation process. The most important examples likely to appear in typical package selections are as follows:

- `exim`, the server program that Debian uses for low-level handling of email messages. If you make a mistake when you install `exim`, you can re-run the `eximconfig` program at any time. There is some advice on simple `exim` configurations in Chapter 8, "Advanced Configuration."
- `gpm`, a tool that provides mouse support when you are using Linux's text console. This has a fairly self-explanatory configuration procedure that detects the type of mouse you are using. But unless you are expecting to use the text console (as opposed to the X Window System, which provides its own mouse support), you may decide you don't want `gpm`.
- `bind`, a program that makes your computer a self-sufficient part of the Internet Domain Name Service. It can be a rather complex program to configure. However, if, like most users, you just want to get name lookups working, accepting the suggested defaults should work fine.
- `apache`, the common UNIX Web server, also provides you with some opportunities for configuration. Once again, unless you are a Web server expert, just accept the defaults—it is easy enough to reconfigure later if you need to.

- X servers, the core part of the X Window system, are also included. Instructions for installing and configuring X are found in Chapter 6, "The First Steps in Debian." Unless you have used Debian before, it is best to bet a base system working first, then set up X later on.

There are various other packages that can request extra information when they are installed. In many cases, this is quite simple: For instance, the installation script for the lynx Web browser will ask for a default web page to visit when you start the browser. The installation scripts are generally helpful when they prompt you for information, and there are usually warnings of any potential problems. But if you want to avoid being asked too many questions all at once, it is best to install a simple Debian base system then add a few packages at a time, rather than installing hundreds of complex packages in a single session.

The remaining options on the menu are less important. If there are any packages that have been partially installed but that were not configured properly, the Config option attempts to fix them. If you use the selection screen to remove some packages, you should choose the Remove option from the main menu to physically delete them from the machine. Unless there are packages awaiting configuration or removal, selecting these options does nothing.

The Selection System

The core of dselect is the Select page, which allows you to browse through the set of available packages (see Figure 5.6). You can scroll up and down through the list using the cursor arrow keys. It is also possible to search for a single package by name. The search function is activated by pressing the / key (a common shortcut used by a number of text-based UNIX programs). The \ key can be used to skip to second and subsequent matches.

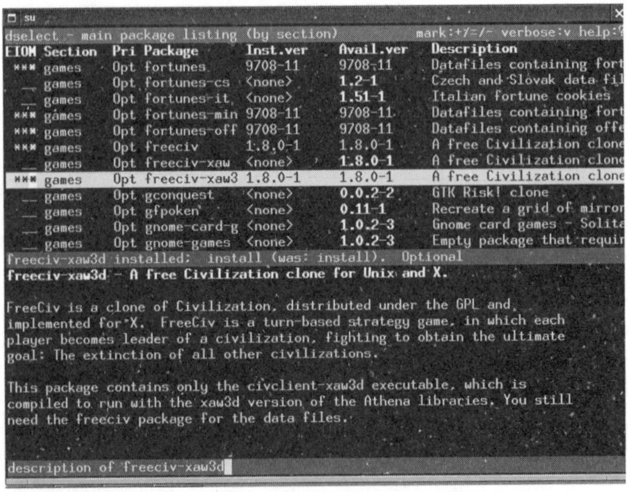

Figure 5.6

The main package selection screen.

When packages are installed, you will see that version numbers for both the installed and newest available packages are shown—if these don't match, dselect upgrades the system to the newer version when you select Install. The columns on the left of the screen indicate the installation status of a package.

A row of three asterisks (***) indicates that a package is installed and set up. The third of these symbols represents the *selected* (as opposed to actual) status of a package: — * means that the package will be added to the system next time you select Install, whereas ** - means that an installed package has been flagged for removal.

Once you are starting to become familiar with Debian, it's worth taking a little time to browse through the full list of packages, and pick out any that might be particularly useful. Pressing the o and O keys allows you to cycle through various schemes of sorting the package listing. If you see a package that interests you, select it with the + key. The - key is used to unselect packages.

Handling Dependencies

Whenever you select or unselect a package, dselect checks the packages dependencies. If the operation you have just performed breaks any dependencies, the program displays a sub-list of packages to help you resolve the problem (see Figure 5.7). When this happens, you can either press Enter to accept dselect's solution to the problem, press X (must be uppercase) to abort the operation completely, or manually select and unselect packages until the problem is solved.

Figure 5.7

The dependency-resolution screen.

The most common situation involves selecting one package that relies on others that haven't been selected. In this case, dselect automatically selects all the required packages, and you can normally just accept this by pressing Enter. Some packages may also *suggest* that you might like to install other packages that complement them—you have a chance to read the descriptions of the suggested packages and see if you agree.

Dependency handling is complicated slightly by the idea of *virtual packages*. These are package names that represent abstract concepts rather than real programs. A typical example is found in the X Window system (see Chapter 6). Various parts of the system rely on a program called an X server, which acts as a kind of driver for your video hardware. However, there are several different X servers, and you must choose the correct one for your particular system.

While X components cannot specify a dependency for any specific X server package, they *do* depend on a virtual xserver package. Any package that provides the xserver capability will satisfy this dependency. If you try to install a program that depends on a virtual package, dselect locates all the real packages providing the required capability, and then prompts you to choose which one to install.

If you remove a package used by some other package, this will obviously trigger a dependency problem too. In this case, you'll probably want to press Shift-X to undo the operation. If you really want to remove the package, you need to remove the packages that depend on it too.

Upgrading Your System

The dselect program can automatically recognize when an available package is newer than the version you currently have installed. This option allows for automatic upgrades. Even once a Debian distribution has been marked as stable, there are sometimes minor updates, generally to fix security-related problems. At the time of writing, the FTP archives carry Debian 2.1r2, which differs by a few packages from the original 2.1 release. Such minor upgrades can be carried out simply by setting your nearest full Debian archive as the package source, and then selecting Update, followed by Install. Note that the package manager is very flexible about where packages come from. Even if you carried out your original installation entirely from CD, there is nothing to stop you from switching your access method to apt and upgrading over the Internet.

The same approach can be used to upgrade from one major release of the distribution to another. But in this case a much greater proportion of the packages must be upgraded, and there may be some significant changes. Package-installation scripts are usually written to ensure that upgrades take place gracefully, but it's best to check your system carefully after an upgrade.

Since a large number of packages change between major versions, unless you have a fast network connection, it is probably worth buying a new CD-ROM set and setting it as your package source. Remember that if you have some new CDs, you need to go through the Access and Update stages again to ensure that the package manager knows about the updated distribution.

If you are using the new `apt` system as your package access method, there is a better method for upgrading to a new distribution version. This alternative method takes extra care to ensure that essential packages are upgraded cleanly. Set up your `apt` source list (using the Access option in `dselect`, for instance), and then type

```
apt-get update
apt-get dist-upgrade
```

Upgrading to a new distribution is one situation where it may be easier to use `apt` even if you are going to be installing a new distribution from CD. To do this, make sure that the `apt-cdrom` package is installed, and read the manual page. You can then add each CD-ROM in your set to the `apt` source list by inserting it and using the command.

```
apt-cdrom add
```

You can then use `apt-get` to upgrade your distribution just as described above.

Taking the Direct Approach

While the `dselect` tool is convenient for browsing the main Debian archives—and potentially any other software archive arranged in the Debian-standard manner—not every program is available this way. Some programs that aren't part of the standard Debian distribution can be downloaded from the program's main Internet site as `.deb` files. Similarly, if you just want a single package from the Debian non-U.S. servers, it can be easier to run a Web browser or FTP tool and download the file yourself rather than set up a package source properly. Package files can be installed by running `dpkg` directly (while logged on as root). For example

```
dpkg -i mypackage_1.00-1.deb
```

The `-i` option tells the system that you want to install the package. The package manager determines if any dependencies are broken, but it is not able to automatically install any extra packages. If you see any package-dependency errors, run `dselect` and search for the required packages. Occasionally, you might see some large application that's supplied as a number of `.deb` files, with some files depending on others. If so, the documentation usually gives some advice on the order of installation.

Packages that have been installed in this way appear in the `dselect` listing under the `Obsolete/local` packages sections. This doesn't mean that there is any problem with the package: It simply tells you that the package was not present in the main Debian archives, and therefore `dselect` is unable to compare the version number of the installed version with the latest available version in the archive. Even if you installed a package manually, you can still use `dselect` if you ever want to remove it again.

It is also possible to invoke the `apt` system from the command line. You have already seen how the `apt-get` command can be used to fetch all the files needed to upgrade your installation to the latest Debian version. It is also possible to use the same program to install or upgrade a single package, for instance

```
apt-get install freeciv
```

Note that `apt-get` can only be invoked with package *names*: You cannot supply the complete filename of a package file. This command searches your `apt` source list (assuming that you have set one up) and locates the most recent package answering to the name of 'freeciv'. This will be installed, together with any other packages which are needed to satisfy its dependencies. Some users prefer to run `apt-get` in this way instead of, or as a complement to, `dselect`.

Installing Non-Debian Software

Virtually all of the most popular Linux software is either included in the standard Debian distribution or available independently as a `.deb` package file. But occasionally you may want to install a program for which no `.deb` file is available. If so, you might find a package in the alternative RPM package format, originally designed by Red Hat for its own distribution, and now adopted by various other distributions.

One approach is to simply use the normal RPM tool (available as a standard Debian package) to install `.rpm` files. Unfortunately, RPM uses its own database for storing information on installed packages and managing package dependencies, so by installing RPMs in this way, you are losing out on many of the benefits of package management. A better approach is to use the `alien` tool to convert the RPMs into Debian packages, which then can be installed as normal using `dpkg`. The alien tool is documented fully on its manual page, but generally you just use a command such as

```
alien —to-deb mypackage-1.00.rpm
```

Sometimes you will also find program source code supplied as a `.rpm` file—these are often called SRPMs. Since the code will always be available as a TAR archive, these are rarely of interest to Debian users. Debian source code distributions do not use a special package format. Instead, the source code is supplied as a standard `tar.gz` file. This is normally accompanied by a small text file with the extension `.dsc`.

Tar Archives

The other common format used for distributing Linux software is the tar archive file. These files are usually compressed using the `gzip` tool (and thus given the suffix `.tar.gz`, or occasionally `.tgz`). Compressed tar files are the UNIX world's equivalent of ZIP archives. These can contain either ready-to-use binary software or the uncompiled source code for a program: Determine which you're getting before you download!

These archives are extracted using commands such as

```
tar -zxvf myprogram.tar.gz
```

See the manual page for `tar` for an explanation of the options used here. Note that, unlike special package files, these archives don't come with any information to tell the system *where* the files they contain should be installed—look for installation instructions for help with this. Sometimes you need to uncompress the archive in a specific directory. In other cases, especially when dealing with large commercial packages, you can uncompress the archive in a temporary location and then run a small program that installs all the other files in their proper places.

Installing from Source Code

Much of the freedom of using free software comes from the fact that the original source code is always available. This is most appealing to users who have some programming experience and thus have the expertise to fix bugs or add new features. But even if you don't program yourself, it is sometimes useful to be able to build packages from the source.

Some more unusual programs are distributed only as source code. The same goes for experimental versions of programs—developers often don't bother to build binary packages if there's going to be a new release in a few days time. Building from source also tends to be more important for users of non-Intel architectures, since the majority of Linux developers have access only to PC-type machines.

To build a package from source code, you need to have a selection of development tools installed—these are described in Chapter 7. Many packages also rely on a number of libraries. As well as the library packages themselves, you need the accompanying development files. These are normally provided in packages with names ending in -dev, and are also described in Chapter 7.

Source code is generally distributed as tar.gz files—uncompress this somewhere convenient using a command such as

```
tar -zxvf mypackage-1.00.tar.gz
```

The source code almost always appears in a directory called mypackage or mypackage-1.00. The method for building source code will vary from package to package, but is normally documented in a file called README or INSTALL in the top-level directory of the package. But a large proportion of modern open source software comes with a GNU-style automatic configuration script—a file called configure in the top-level directory. If this file is present, you can usually prepare the program for building by changing into the package's top-level directory and then running the configure script:

```
./configure
```

This script searches the system to ensure that all libraries and tools required by the build process are installed. If all goes well, you can then start the build process itself just by typing

```
make
```

For a major package, compilation could take some time. When it is complete, you can install the program in its normal place with the following command:

```
su -c "make install"
```

You will then be prompted to enter the system's root password. The su program is being used here to run a single command (enclosed between quotes after the –c option) with root privileges. In this case, root privileges are needed so that your new program can be installed in the main system package directories, which aren't writable by normal users.

Summary

In this chapter, you have seen how to use the `dselect` package management front-end to complete your Debian installation. The same program can be used at any time to add and remove packages from your system. As well as making it easy to install a wide range of GNU/Linux software, the Debian package system works to keep you in control of the software installed on your machine: It is easy to remove or upgrade packages at any time. The programs of the package management system also help you to avoid any problems relating to package dependencies.

If you have been installing or upgrading your Debian system over a network, you will already be using the `apt` system to fetch package files. In future versions of Debian, you will use the same system to install packages which are supplied on CD: You can already try this out by using the `apt-cdrom` command to add Debian CDs to your `apt` source list. As well as working with `dselect`, the `apt` system can be used directly from the command line, and serves as the foundation for new package management front-ends, notably `gnome-apt`.

Having read this chapter and completed your first Debian installation, you are ready to start doing real work with your GNU/Linux system. The following chapters will help you turn a basic installation into a powerful and productive system.

CHAPTER 6

The First Steps in Debian

In this chapter, you begin to look at some of the major facilities available on your new Debian system. This chapter, together with the next two, covers the configuration and use of some of the most important subsystems and programs available on a GNU/Linux machine. This chapter concentrates in particular on the X Window System, the common graphical user interface for UNIX-like operating systems.

With the installation completed, the first thing you see is a text-console login prompt, which will look something like

```
Debian GNU/Linux 2.1 adzel tty1

adzel login:
```

You should have created a normal account for yourself during the install procedure, so log on using this username to start experimenting with your system. When you are using a Linux system in text mode, you have several *virtual consoles* available—these have already been mentioned in connection with the Debian installer. Now that the full system is up and running, you can use them to run several login sessions at the same time. For instance, if you want to do some system-management operations, you can switch to the second console using Alt+F2 and then log on again as root.

A Word About Configuration Files

Traditionally, UNIX systems have always been configured using human-readable text files. Under Debian, there are a number of helpful scripts and tools that can automate the management of some of these files, but ultimately you still need to edit some of them by hand. This isn't as difficult as it sounds—

most of the files contain comment lines explaining what each section does. And you always have the option of making a backup copy of the file before you start.

If you have ever used a UNIX system before, you will probably already have some views about text editors. Most of the popular UNIX editors are included in the standard Debian distribution, so just run `dselect` and search for your favorite one. If you haven't used a UNIX system before, now is the time to look into the available editors. The "Text Editors" section in Chapter 7, "A Tour of the Packages," compares some of the better-known UNIX editors. When in doubt, start off by looking at the emacs editor, which was developed as the standard editor for the GNU project. The emacs editor is an incredibly powerful program; short descriptions of some simple editing operations in emacs appear in the "First Steps in GNU Emacs" sidebar that follows.

Since UNIX is a multiuser system, some programs have two kinds of configuration files. Systemwide configuration files are customarily stored in the /etc directory. In the case of programs that provide system services, this will normally be the only configuration file. But for tools such as mail readers, which are run by individual users, each user can often keep a personal configuration file in his or her home directory. The values in the personal configuration file override the systemwide defaults. Configuration files in the home directory normally have names starting with a period. This means that the `ls` command, and many graphical file-management tools, will not normally display them. To list all files in a directory, including those starting with a ., use the command

```
ls -a
```

FIRST STEPS IN GNU EMACS

To install emacs, just search the `dselect` package list for the `emacs20` package, and press + to select it. You may find an older version of GNU Emacs, plus several other emacs-like editors, available. These are basically similar, but may include different user interfaces.

One of the main advantages of GNU Emacs is that it runs well in both text-only and windowed modes—the program automatically detects whether or not a windowed environment is available when you start it (Figure 6.1 shows the windowed variant). In either mode, there is a menu bar along the top of the screen. In windowed mode, the menus can simply be pulled down using the mouse, while in full-screen mode you must press F10 to activate the menu system and then use the arrow keys to select menu items.

The editor can be started from the command line just by typing **emacs** (like almost all UNIX commands, this is all lowercase). Normally, you specify a filename after the command. If this file exists, it will be edited immediately; otherwise it will be created. Alternatively, you can open new files at any time using the menu system.

A single copy of emacs can have several files open at one time, each appearing in a separate editor buffer. You can switch between them using the Buffers menu or a variety of keyboard shortcuts.

Technically, emacs is described as a modeless screen editor. What this means in practice is that you can position the cursor using the arrow keys or mouse and then insert text simply by typing—note that this is *not* true of some of the other popular UNIX editors. Once you have finished, select Save Buffer from the Files menu, or simply quit the program and answer **y** when asked if you want to save your edited file.

Needless to say, there are hundreds of other commands (try Control+K to delete a line, for instance, and Control+Shift to activate the Undo feature). The complete emacs package also contains numerous sub-programs, including a special browser system for its own manual. If you like emacs and want to learn how to get the most from it, start by browsing the online tutorial available from the Help menu.

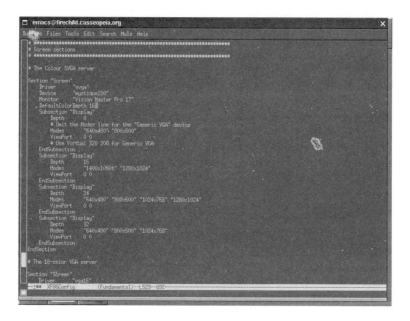

Figure 6.1

GNU Emacs running in the X Window System.

You have already encountered UNIX manual pages that cover the key programs of a GNU Linux system. There are also pages that document the format of many important configuration files. For instance, you can view documentation of the configuration file for the LILO Linux Loader by typing

```
man lilo.conf
```

Configuration file formats are documented in section 5 of the manual. Sometimes, the same keyword can have entries in more than one manual section. To look up `lilo.conf` in section 5 of the manual, ignoring all other sections, you can type

```
man 5 lilo.conf
```

There are nine sections to the manual, each with its own significance. The full list is shown here:

1. Standard commands and applications, including all the everyday programs like `ls` and `man`.
2. System calls (the programmer's interface to the Linux kernel).
3. Functions provided by programmers' libraries.
4. Special files, which are mainly the device files in the `/dev` directory.
5. File formats, especially configuration files.
6. Games and entertainment programs.
7. Text markup systems, where the file format of the manual pages is described.
8. System administration programs.
9. Internal documentation of the Linux kernel. This is the one section that you won't find in other UNIX systems. It will generally be of interest only if you want to write a new device driver or otherwise modify the kernel.

Setting Up a Graphical User Interface

Unlike some other systems, Linux doesn't make the windowed user interface a core part of the operating system. Instead, graphical functions are provided by a set of normal application programs that run on top of the OS kernel just like any other tool. This means that there is no need to run a GUI on a machine that is going to sit in a corner working as a server. Additionally, it makes it possible to replace part or all of the GUI system with a new design without touching core OS functions.

Currently, all popular UNIX GUIs are based on the X Window System, sometimes abbreviated to X11 or just X. The X Window System is a flexible modular windowing environment. There are three classes of programs that together make up a complete X system:

- **The X display server**. This is a kind of device driver for your graphics card. It manages a display that acts as a canvas on which the rest of the system can draw windows and other graphics. As a Linux user, you use one of the X servers developed by the XFree86 project.
- **The window manager**. This is a special program that interacts with the X server and performs functions that create the look and feel of the systems—notably the drawing of window borders. There is a wide selection of window managers available. Some of these will look familiar to users of Windows or MacOS. Others, such as the popular Enlightenment system, offer an easily configurable appearance. Some Enlightenment configurations look quite outlandish, although they may be something of an acquired taste. Unless otherwise stated, all figures of X applications in this book were taken with the popular GNU WindowMaker window manager running.

- **X clients**. These are the everyday applications of the X Window System—anything from a clock to a word processor.

Since X is a network-aware windowing system, clients don't actually need to be running on the same computer as the X server. While you normally won't need this flexibility for simple installations, it can sometimes be useful if you have a private network. Some people find the client-server terminology used in relation to the X Window System a little confusing. You will always run an X server on your workstation machine. But X clients can run either on your workstation or on some other machine (see Figure 6.2). From a user's point of view, a remote machine on which an application runs is normally considered a server, so in X terminology, the client and server may appear to be reversed.

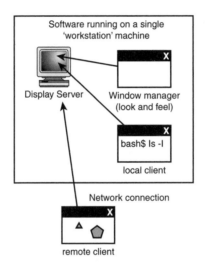

Figure 6.2

The relationship between an X client and the display server. The window manager is a special client that controls the appearance of all other clients.

The logic behind this arrangement is that when an X client application starts up, it establishes a network connection to a display server (which may be either local or remote). This connection resembles the situation when a Web browser (client) opens a connection to fetch a document from a Web server. Thus, the key issue is the direction in which the network connection is established. For discussion of the practicalities of running X applications over a network, see Chapter 10, "Exploring the X Window System."

Installing the X Window System

Before you can use the X Window System, you need to install an X server, a window manager, and various support packages. The first thing to decide is which server to install. Start by finding out as much as you can about your video card: the manufacturer and model and, if possible, the type of chipset it uses.

The best way to find the right X server is to run dselect, enter the package selection screen, press / to invoke the search function, and then type **xserver**. You will see a list of available X server packages. You might see an X server that specifically supports your chipset. If not, take a look at the xserver-svga package as well as at old SVGA cards.

If you have trouble deciding which X server to use, try looking at the XFree86 Web site at http://www.xfree86.org/.

Alternatively, install the xserver-common package and then read the documentation files installed in /usr/doc/xserver-common.

When you select an X server package, dselect will pick up dependencies for several other packages—these are libraries and essential programs for the X Window System. At the same time, you must also install some fonts for the system. If in doubt, install all the xfonts packages. When you install an X server, the installation script asks you if you want to make this server the default. Obviously you will want to respond with a yes.

NOTE

The XFree86 developers have been working for some time on version 4 of its X server system. Due to some major design changes, it is likely that there will just be a single server, which should work almost any graphics chipsets.

Once you have the core X packages selected, you should choose a window manager. You may want to experiment with several but, when in doubt, start off with WindowMaker (provided in the wmaker Debian package). This manager offers a good balance between efficient use of resources and an attractive (and configurable) appearance. When you install a window manager, you are asked if you want to make it the default. This just means that it will be used if you start an X session without manually specifying which window manager to use. With a little configuration, each user on the system can override the default—see the section "Setting Up an X Session Script" later in this chapter.

While you are selecting packages, you might also want to install other X client applications. At an absolute minimum, you will want the xterm package. But there are hundreds more windowed applications to choose from, ranging from small tools like xdaliclock to huge applications such as gimp. For a list of other applications, see Chapter 7 or just start browsing the dselect package list.

Configuring the X Server

Having installed an X server that suits your system, you should now configure it. XFree86 servers are configured by the file /etc/X11/XF86Config. This file can be edited by hand, but you can usually create a suitable file by running the xf86config tool. This is a text-based tool, but it provides comprehensive help messages that explain all the key options and guide you through the process.

The main items you need to configure in your X server setup files are as follows:

- Mouse details
- Keyboard layout
- The specifications of your monitor
- Some details of your video card (more important if you have an old card)
- The selection of screen resolutions that you want to use

First you are asked to specify which type of mouse (or other pointing device) you are using. Some X applications rely on your having a three-button mouse. If you have a two-button mouse, it is worth accepting the Emulate3Buttons option. This allows you to simulate a click with the middle button by pressing both buttons simultaneously. But if you use applications that need a third button extensively, you might find that it's worth getting a proper three-button mouse.

You also need to enter the Linux device name of the mouse. If you are using a PS/2 mouse attached to the system auxiliary port, this name will be /dev/psaux. If you have a serial mouse, you must specify the appropriate serial port. If it is attached to the first serial port (COM1 under Windows), the Linux name is /dev/ttyS0. COM2 becomes /dev/ttyS1.

Next comes keyboard configuration—just follow through the menus and you should see options that suit your keyboard layout and native language. If there aren't any options that suit your native language, try to select the nearest match, and then contact a local Linux user who has the same keyboard arrangements and ask for advice.

Now you need to tell the X server something about the capabilities of the monitor. The important numbers are the maximum and minimum values for the horizontal and vertical sync rates of the screen display. The user's manual for your monitor usually includes a specifications section that provides the appropriate values, and you can just enter these when prompted. If you are stuck, look at the list of values the xf86config program prints, and pick the options that match the screen mode you normally use under Windows.

Having entered these, you are asked to enter a name for the monitor record, which is stored in the XF86Config file. This isn't particularly important, so you can just press Return, thus allowing the program to use a default value.

You also need to enter some information about the video card you are using. First, you are asked which X server you intend to run—you should already have decided this, installed the appropriate server, and made it the default. Next, you must tell the program how much video memory your card has. As with the monitor settings, you are asked to give a name for your video card definition, but once again it is safe to just accept the defaults.

The program also prompts you to select which kind of clock chip is present on the card. For all except a few relatively old cards, there is no need to set anything here; press Return to skip this section.

The final step is to configure the range of available screen resolutions. There is a separate list of resolutions for each color depth. When you first start XFree86, you will normally be using the 8-bit per pixel color depth, so at the very least you should make sure that you have a sensible selection of resolutions for this color depth.

If you set more than one resolution, the first resolution in the list is used when the X server starts. You can then switch to other resolutions on this list by pressing Control and Alt together with either the + or the - key on the numeric keypad.

NOTE

If you have selected more than one screen resolution, note that when you switch between them you only change the amount that is shown on the screen, *not* the size of your desktop (which never changes during an X session). When the desktop area is larger than the selected screen resolution, the *virtual area* facility of XFree86 is activated; your desktop will scroll when you move the pointer to the edges of the screen. If you find this disconcerting, ensure that you have not configured any screen resolutions larger than what you normally use.

If you want to tune the /etc/X11/XF86Config file manually—for instance, to alter the selection of screen modes available without running xf86config again—start by reading the manual page for XF86Config. This page provides comprehensive information about the file format. Many of the options you are likely to want to change are in the Screen section of the file. Note that there are actually four of these sections: one used by monochrome servers, one by the 16-color VGA driver, one for SVGA, and one called Accelerated, which is used by all the other X server packages. Be sure to edit the right section for the server you are using, otherwise you won't see any changes. Note that the use of the term Accelerated is now rather confusing—in recent versions of

XFree86, the SVGA server can take advantage of graphics acceleration features present in many cards.

One option you probably want to change manually is the color depth the X server will use. When XFree86 servers start up, they normally default to 8-bit per pixel color (256 colors)—obviously excepting the monochrome and 16-color VGA servers. With modern graphics cards, you most likely want a 16bpp (65,000 colors) or 24bpp (16.7 million colors) display. There are various ways you can make the server start with different color depths, but the easiest way is to edit /etc/X11/XF86Config, locate the Screen section for the server you are using, and add a line such as

```
DefaultColorDepth    16
```

Starting an X Session

When you think the X server is set up correctly, log on using your normal account and start your first X session by running the startx command. The screen should clear, and then the X server runs, accompanied by your default window manager. Exactly what you do next depends on the window manager. WindowMaker and many others provide a menu of useful programs if you right-click the desktop background (called the root window in X terminology). The WindowMaker root window menu is shown in Figure 6.3. Try running the xterm program—this program gives you a normal UNIX command-line interpreter (shell) in a window, and you can run all your usual command-line tools here.

If you have installed some X applications, you may find that they already appear on the root window menu. Most window manager packages supplied with Debian automatically generate the menu to reflect the programs currently available. Alternatively, you can run programs from the shell prompt in an xterm. For example

```
emacs myfile.txt &
```

NOTE

Notice the & character at the end of the command line. It is used to run emacs under X. This is standard shorthand that tells the shell to start the program running as a background job. If you omit the ampersand , the shell will wait until you have quit emacs before letting you type another command. You almost always want to use & when running X applications from the command line.

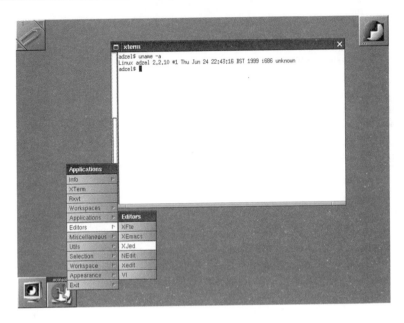

Figure 6.3

A simple WindowMaker session. The root window menu is a common feature of most modern window managers.

When you want to finish your X session, the normal approach is to kill the window manager. Most window managers provide an Exit option in their root window menus. When you select this option, the whole X session terminates and you are returned to the text console. If you have chosen a default window manager that doesn't have an easy escape route, you can forcibly terminate the session by pressing Control+Alt+Backspace—but use this as a last resort.

You can also switch out of X temporarily using the virtual console system. Just pressing Alt and a function key doesn't work when X is running, but Control+Alt+F1 will take you to virtual console 1. When you want to switch back, you'll find the X session running on virtual console 7.

Setting Up an X Session Script

By default, when you start a new X session, Debian just loads the system default window manager, with no other applications. But it is easy to override this behavior—if the system detects a file called .xsession in your home directory, it will use this to configure your session instead.

The .xsession file is normally a Bourne shell script and, if you are familiar with UNIX scripting, there is almost no limitation to what you can do from this file. But in most cases, you will just want to run a few applications and a window manager (which may or may not be the system default). A typical file might look like this:

```
# .xsession file for thomas@adzel

xterm -bg black -fg wheat &
xdaliclock &
exec WindowMaker
```

As with any shell script, lines beginning with a # character are treated as comments and ignored. The next two lines are normal command lines for starting X client applications—note the & character at the end of each line to signify that the program runs in the background. This particular file starts an xterm (with some options specifying background and foreground colors) and a clock program.

The final line in any .xsession file is rather special. It should always start some program (in this case the WindowMaker window manager), but it is run in a different way: The exec command is used, and there is no & character. This makes the program started in this way the *session manager*. The X session will continue for as long as its session manager program is running and then exit silently.

It is common practice to make the window manager the session manager. This means that the session will end when you select Exit from the window manager menu. But you can make any program the session manager. If you are using an application-launching panel (such as the panels supplied with the various desktop environment packages, described later), you might prefer to make this the session manager instead. In this case, you can use a file like this:

```
# .xsession file with a panel utility as session manager

xdaliclock &
WindowMaker &
exec panel
```

Every .xsession file should start one (and only one) window manager—even if it is not going to be used as your session manager. Strictly speaking, it *is* possible to use the X Window System without a window manager, but this is graphically unattractive and rather difficult—you will have difficulty moving, resizing, and closing windows, since these facilities are normally provided by the window manager.

Occasionally, you may encounter an error in your X session file. This error could result in some of the applications failing to start, or even in the whole session exiting prematurely. If so, look for any error messages that might have been produced while running the .xsession file—these errors are logged in a file called .xsession-errors, also located in your home directory.

Desktop Environments

The core X Window System provides an environment in which to run windowed applications. But it does not, on its own, provide a wide selection of utilities that might be familiar to users of other windowed user interfaces. The definition of a desktop environment is rather vague—it can applied to any package that provides a selection of everyday graphical tools with a common look and feel. For many people, the most important component of a good desktop environment is a graphical file manager.

For some years, many UNIX systems have been supplied with the Common Desktop Environment (CDE). The CDE tools run on Linux-based systems, but this is a commercial (and quite expensive) product and won't be considered here. In recent years, there have been several open source projects to develop new desktop environments for the X Window System. The GNOME and K Desktop Environment (KDE) projects have both produced a variety of high quality software programs.

In some UNIX and Linux forums, you may encounter heated discussions of the merits of the desktop environments. In fact, there is no particular reason why you need to choose one over the other—it is entirely possible to have both installed on each machine, and to run your favorite programs from each. Efforts are underway to make the two systems work together even better—in the future, they will both use the same mechanisms to support drag and drop data transfers, for instance. But if there is a certain degree of rivalry between the two camps, it only serves to fuel the development of both systems.

GNOME

For those who care, GNOME is actually the GNU Network Object Model Environment—a name that reflects technology used to allow sophisticated interaction between the components of the system (similar methods are also being used in the KDE project, as it happens). Details of the project, regular news announcements, and some screenshots can all be found at the main Web site at http://www.gnome.org/.

GNOME doesn't specify a standard window manager, although Enlightenment and WindowMaker are both popular choices. What you do get are the desktop environment essentials: a handy configurable application-launching panel and a graphical file manager called gmc (see Figure 6.4), plus a host of extras ranging from a dedicated help browser to a windowed implementation of the standard UNIX talk system. GNOME project members are also working on a variety of bigger applications, including the balsa email client and the powerful gnumeric spreadsheet. And to complete your desktop, there are a few games including the obligatory mine-hunting puzzle.

A final version of GNOME is a part of the main distribution for Debian 2.2. Debian 2.1 *does* include some GNOME packages, but they are based on a prerelease version and are best avoided now that full release versions are available. If you want to try GNOME on a Debian 2.1 system or ensure that you have the latest version, you can add the project's FTP site as an APT package source. This way, the packages will be available in your standard package selection. There are instructions for doing this on the project Web site.

GNOME is supplied as a large number of package files—most of the major applications are provided separately. This means you only need to install the tools you like. But the main GNOME packages depend on a huge array of support libraries. If you are using dselect to install them, all the required libraries should be picked up automatically. If you are downloading and installing packages manually, check the installation instructions on the Web site.

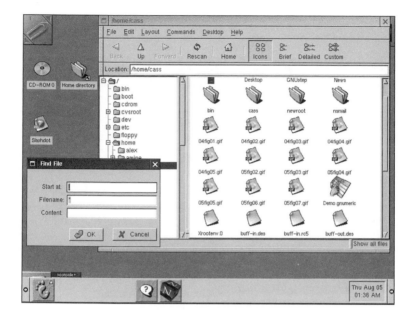

Figure 6.4

The GNOME Midnight Commander file management system is one of the key components of the desktop environment.

When you have installed all the GNOME packages you want, edit your .xsession file to look something like this:

```
# .xsession file which runs GNOME Midnight commander and
# the GNOME panel

WindowMaker &
gmc &
exec panel
```

Note that this makes the GNOME application-launching panel your X session manager. To end the section, select the Log Off option from the panel, rather than exiting the window manager.

KDE

The main alternative to the GNOME tools is offered by the KDE project (which actually predates GNOME slightly). Again, it provides a wide range of tools, from the kfm file manager (which also works as a credible Web browser), to useful little tools such as kljettool (for configuring LaserJet-series printers). The system also includes its own window manager, which gives a look and feel rather reminiscent of Windows (see Figure 6.5). But, of course, you can use a different window manager if you prefer. Incidentally, don't bother looking for a hidden meaning in the initial K—the developers claim that it really doesn't stand for anything.

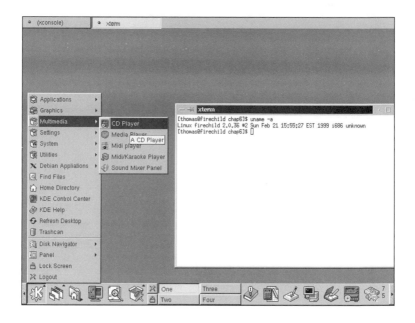

Figure 6.5

A typical KDE desktop, using the K Window Manager.

The KDE developers are also working on a number of major productivity applications, which together make up the KOffice suite. These include the KWord word processor and the KIllustrator vector graphics package. For progress reports on these, see `http://koffice.kde.org/`.

KDE isn't a standard part of the Debian distribution. But the KDE project team compiles Debian packages of each release, and these are easy to download and install— look at the main KDE Web site to find your nearest mirror of the archive site. While KDE is split into a number of components, the packaging is not as fine-grained as GNOME. Even so, check the latest installation instructions on the Web site for advice on the order in which you install the packages. Do watch out for the requirement of the Qt user interface toolkit. This isn't always available from the same place as the KDE packages themselves, but it *is* provided in the standard Debian archives, so when in doubt just install it with `dselect` before you start.

Having installed KDE, you can try the complete system by creating a minimal `.xsession` file that looks like this:

```
# .xsession file which runs KDE
exec startkde
```

startkde is a script (normally installed in the directory /usr/X11R6/bin) that starts all the main KDE components. This is itself a valid .xsession file. So if you decide that you like some of the components but, for instance, you want a different window manager, try making your .xsession file a copy of the startkde file, then edit it to run the parts you want.

Setting Up a Graphical Login Screen

If you use windowed applications occasionally, you can keep the default system of logging on a text console and then starting an X session using the startx command whenever you need one. But today, almost everyone uses windowed environments routinely. So you might prefer to run an X server automatically when your Debian system starts up, and start an X session immediately when you log on. There are a number of tools, called *display managers*, that start an X server and provide graphical login screens.

The traditional display manager is called xdm, and it is one of the core tools of the X Window System. This display manager has a number of configuration options, but most of these are only relevant when the machine is running in a complex client-server environment. To use the display manager, just run dselect and install the xdm package. You can test the program simply by logging on as root and typing **xdm**. You should see a login screen. After entering your normal username and password, you will see your normal X session. The xdm package automatically integrates into the Debian init system and will start whenever the machine boots.

The xdm display manager works fine, but its appearance is, at best, functional. If you want to beautify your system a little, there are now several alternatives around. The GNOME project provides the gdm display manager—like xdm, just install the relevant package and it will automatically start up when the machine boots. As well as a more modern appearance, gdm adds some extra features, notably menu options that allow you to shut down or reboot the machine without manually typing commands.

The KDE developers have also produced their own solution, called (surprisingly enough) kdm. Unless you know exactly what you're doing, don't try installing more than one display manager at a time; they can clash with each other.

Managing User Accounts

Linux was designed from the ground up as a multiuser operating system. This means that the owner of every file on your disks, and every program running on the system, is recorded. Whenever a program attempts to access a file, the kernel first checks that it has permission to do so. Even if you have a single user account on the machine, this check is still valuable—since all the key system files are owned by the root account, you must specifically log on as root before you modify them, thus avoiding the risk of accidental modifications.

But the multiuser capabilities really come into their own if your computer is to be used by family or colleagues. Users can keep their own personal files private. And since major UNIX applications read their configuration from files in users' home directories, users can all set up their accounts to meet their personal requirements without interfering with anyone else's options.

The UNIX security model actually involved two kinds of ownership—user ownership and group ownership. Both users and groups are represented internally by numerical IDs, but in practice you will normally use names. User and group IDs are mapped to names in the files /etc/passwd and /etc/group. Despite its name, /etc/passwd doesn't necessarily contain any password data. If, as suggested, you accepted the shadow passwords option during installation, passwords will be stored (in encrypted form) in the file /etc/shadow. This arrangement is considered more secure, since it means that the encrypted password file isn't readable by ordinary users on the system. Even though they are encrypted, having them on public display is an unnecessary risk.

Each file on a UNIX file system has both a user ID and a group ID. Each user is a member of one or more groups. On a Debian system, each user account normally has a corresponding group of the same name, and this is the primary group for the account. This means that a file created by a user logged on as thomas will have a user ID of thomas and a group of thomas—although these can be changed using the chown command.

On large system, administrators sometimes create extra groups, allowing all users who work on a particular project to access shared files. A new group can be created using the addgroup command. The group mechanism can also be used to control access to a particular system resource. There are several standard groups created automatically during the installation for this purpose. For instance, on a standard Debian system, access to any sound hardware installed is restricted to users in the audio group. Similarly, you can give a user permission to activate a dial-up Internet connection by adding them to the dip group. This particular case is discussed further in Chapter 8, "Advanced Configuration." There are also a number of special groups involved in the normal functioning of specific applications; these are described in the application documentation.

In principle, you can perform all your account management functions by directly editing /etc/passwd and /etc/group. But Debian provides a number of tools that make managing accounts even simpler. The most important of these is the adduser command. This command creates the first user account during installation, and it can be used at any time to create new accounts. For instance

```
adduser thomas
```

You are prompted to enter various personal details about the new user (these can be inspected using the finger command) and an initial login password for the new account. Accounts without passwords are considered bad policy, even on standalone machines, and adduser does not allow the creation of such accounts. The program will then set up the account and a corresponding group and create a new home directory—

which in this case would be called /home/thomas. New home directories are created as a copy of the skeleton directory, /etc/skel. If you are setting up a large number of accounts, this mechanism can be useful for providing standard basic configuration files for all users.

When the adduser command is invoked with a second argument, it adds an existing user to the specified group. For instance, you can allow an account to control dial-up Internet access using this command:

```
adduser thomas dip
```

There is also a variety of commands for changing details of user accounts. To change the password on an account, use the passwd command. If a normal user forgets his or her password, you can log on using the root account and then type

```
passwd <username>
```

This allows you to forcibly change the password of the account. But if you forget the root password, you are in trouble—to get a new root shell you will need to boot from a rescue disk. But try to remember the password. If you are worried about forgetting it, write it down and keep it in a safe place. But remember, anyone who has the root password will have complete access to any part of the system.

File Ownership and Permissions

Most file systems provide a degree of access control—DOS allows you to protect files from overwriting and deleting. But because UNIX systems are designed for multiuser operation, the access control systems are much more sophisticated. To see ownership and access control data for your files, use the -l option for the ls command. This option provides output looking something like this:

```
-rw-r—r—   1 thomas   thomas     146689 Jul 10 11:07 may.jpg
```

The first column gives the file's access restrictions—called the *mode* in UNIX terminology. You then see the owning user, the owning group, the size of the file (in bytes), and the time of last modification. Ownership of the file can be changed using the chown command. For example

```
chown david.coders may.jpg
```

This command sets the file to have owner david and group coders.

The file's access mode consists of three parts. The first part applies to the file's owner, the second part applies to users who don't own the file but who are members of the group that owns the file, and the third part applies to all other users. For each type of user, there are three possible kinds of access: read, write, and execute . The modes of a file are changed using the chmod command. For instance, to allow other group members to read and execute a file, use this:

```
chmod g+rx myfile
```

and to stop users in the others class writing to a file, use this:

```
chmod o-w myfile
```

The default mode of files created by most applications under Debian allows reading and writing by the owner and other group members, and reading only by other users. If you want new files created with some other mode, consult the manual page for the umask command.

For executable (program) files, there are some extra access modes: setuid and setgid. Normally, when a program is started, it runs with the user and group IDs of the user who ran it. But if the program is marked as setuid, it is instead run using the user ID that owns the file. Similarly, setgid programs gain the file's group ID. The most common examples of this kind of program are setuid root system tools. These tools allow normal users limited access to system administrative functions.

For instance, under certain circumstances discussed in Chapter 8, normal users may be allowed to mount new file systems. To achieve this, the mount command is made setuid root, and it becomes the command's responsibility to check whether the user is actually allowed to perform the desired operation. Unless you are a programmer or are performing some complex system management work, you won't need to create new setuid or setgid files. However, you should be aware that they exist and that they are extremely critical to the security of the system. A good majority of the UNIX-related security alerts involves bugs that allow an abuse of the privileged status of a setuid program.

ACCESS BY NUMBERS

So far, you have looked at file access modes as sequences of letters, where each letter specifies that some particular type of file access is allowed. Internally, UNIX file systems represent each file's mode as a single number. You may see these numbers appearing in more advanced Linux documentation. It is possible to use a numerical mode as a parameter for the chmod command. For example

```
chmod 0644 myfile.dat
```

Once you are familiar with numerical modes, you may find them more convenient than the alphabetic style of chmod command.

A numerical mode is a four-digit *octal* number. This means that only the digits 0 to 7 are allowed. The first digit of the number specifies the setuid and setgid flags of the file. For most normal files, you will want to leave this set to zero. The three remaining digits specify access permissions for the file's owner, members of the file's group, and all other users, respectively. The correct value of a digit is obtained by adding the following values together:

4 Read access

2 Write access

1 Permission to execute the file

So, to give read/write access exclusively to the owner, you use mode 0600. To allow everyone to read and execute a file but give only the owner permission to modify it, mode 0755 is appropriate.

Printing—A UNIX Approach

At some point, you will probably produce some documents on your Debian system that you want to print. Virtually all home and small office printers today attach to the computer's parallel port. The raw printer device file (equivalent to LPT1: under Windows) is /dev/lp1, and you can test your printer by logging on as root and sending some text directly to that device. For example

```
cat myfile.txt >/dev/lp1
```

However, there are two drawbacks to using the parallel port device directly for everyday printing. First, the traditional UNIX reasoning: If more than one user tries to access a single printer device at the same time, the second user will find the device busy. If you are using your Debian system as a standalone workstation, you might not think this is an important consideration. But if you ever set up an office print server, it certainly does matter. As a consequence, the default system setup does not allow normal users to directly access parallel devices.

The standard solution to this issue is the lpr package, which manages a queue of print jobs. For simple setups, you can print a file using a command like this:

```
lpr myfile.txt
```

If the printer is currently switched on and not busy, the file will print immediately. But if not, it will be added to a queue and printed as soon as possible. You can see the items in the print queue using the lpq command and cancel a print job using lprm. Note that most windowed UNIX programs offering a print facility generate PostScript files internally and then automatically feed the data into the lpr program.

The second issue when setting up a Linux printing system is that the data sent to the printer must match what the printer is expecting. Printing plain text isn't too much of a problem, but different types of printers expect graphical data in different formats. Presenting graphical data in the correct format is the main function of printer drivers under Windows.

UNIX programs, on the other hand, traditionally output print jobs using the PostScript page description language. Top-of-the-range printers often understand PostScript data directly, and these pose no problem. But PostScript-compatible printers are expensive, and few home users have them. Fortunately, there is a free package called gs (short for Ghostscript) that can convert PostScript files into the data format used by a wide range of printers. It can also preview PostScript (and the related file format, PDF) onscreen.

In an ideal world, a program would inspect all files that you try to print and run gs, or any other appropriate filter program, in order to convert the files to a type understood by your printer. The `magicfilter` package attempts to provide this kind of service. With this package correctly installed, you should be able to print PostScript, PDF, plain text, and a variety of other file formats without needing to run the required filter program manually.

Setting Up a Print System

As so often is the case in the UNIX world, there are many options available when configuring a printer. But the simplest solution for a Debian system is as follows. First of all, you should run `dselect` and ensure that the following packages are installed:

- `lpr`
- `gs`
- `gs-fonts`
- `magicfilter`

You must now set up the `lpr` configuration file, `/etc/printcap` (so-called because it defines the capabilities of printers). This file defines a job queue for your printer device and ensures that files in the print queue are processed through the magic filter before sending them to the printer. If you don't already have an `/etc/printcap` file, the printer configuration program will be run automatically when you install the `magic-filter` package. If this doesn't happen, or if you want to reconfigure the printing system, type

```
magicfilterconfig —force
```

You are asked to provide full and short names for your printer. These aren't too important unless you have more than one printer connected. The default printer device, `/dev/lp1`, will usually be correct. The main choice you need to make is the filter file you wish to use. The program displays a list of the available options, and if you can see one that fits the printer you are using, life becomes easy. If not, you may need to experiment. Remember that many modern printers emulate the HP LaserJet series. Your printer manual may contain some helpful information.

With your `/etc/printcap` file set up, you should be able to use the `lpr` command to print both plain text files and PostScript documents. Normally, the only argument needed by the `lpr` command is the name of the file to print. But if you have more than one printer set up, you can use the `-P` option. For example

```
lpr -Pdeskjet mydocument.ps
```

For a good test, try printing a document from a program such as Netscape or AbiWord. These programs generate PostScript data that should be recognized by the `magicfilter` system and rendered using `gs`. The Print dialog box of Netscape (see Figure 6.6) is a good example of dialog boxes provided by most major UNIX applications. The most important option is the command that should be executed in order to print a PostScript file. If you need to pass any options to the `lpr` command, you can specify them here.

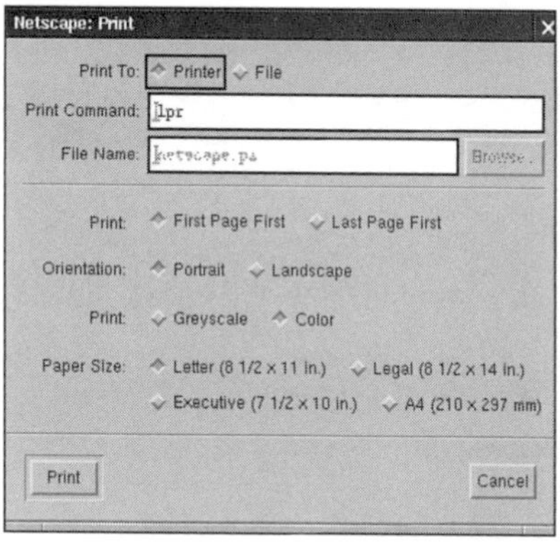

Figure 6.6

UNIX applications allow you to specify the command used to print the document.

If none of the standard filter files seem to suit your printer, you might be able to write your own. The main consideration will normally be whether gs is capable of converting PostScript to a format that suits your printer. You can see a list of output formats by typing

gs -?

If your printer is included on this list but isn't supported by the magicfilter system, copy one of the existing filter files in the /etc/magicfilter directory and modify it to invoke gs with your appropriate printer type. When in doubt, look at the manual pages for magicfilter and gs.

Summary

After working through this chapter, you should have a working windowed environment on your Debian system. Remember that the X Window System is highly configurable. If you don't like the appearance or behavior of the basic installation described here, you will probably be able to change it by reconfiguring the window manager or installing a different one. There is more information about configuring X in Chapter 10.

If you are new to UNIX systems, you should now be more comfortable with the ideas of file ownership and access modes. This chapter also covered the basic steps for configuring a printer attached to your Debian machine. If your computer is networked, you may also want to read the section on networked printers in Chapter 9, "Life on a Network."

CHAPTER 7

A Tour of the Packages

In this chapter, you look at some of the more popular pieces of application software that you might want to use with your Debian system. The chapter coverage concentrates on various important tasks that you are likely to encounter in day-to-day computing, and suggests popular solutions. But there is a huge range of more specialized software included in the Debian distribution, and even more that can be freely downloaded. So if you want something that isn't listed in this chapter, it's worth browsing through the Debian package list to find it.

If you want to keep up to date with the latest software releases for GNU/Linux systems (and other UNIX-like operating systems too, although there is a Linux bias), a good place to start is the Freshmeat Web site at http://freshmeat.net/.

This site allows you to browse through a list of recent GNU/Linux software releases. It gives a short description of each package, plus links to the home page and primary download sites. There is also a search facility to help you track down the program you are looking for.

There are also some documentation packages that you might find interesting. Particularly helpful are a series of documents called HOWTOs that document specific tasks, from setting up an awkward sound card to configuring support for Finnish. These HOWTOs are available in plain text format in the doc-linux-text package, and are installed in the /usr/doc/HOWTO directory. Like many documentation files under Debian, they are compressed using the gzip tool. To read them, use a command such as

```
gzip -dc /usr/doc/HOWTO/IPCHAINS-HOWTO.gz ¦ less
```

The first part of the command decompresses the file so that it is readable. The uncompressed file is then *piped* into `less`, a common UNIX utility that allows you to browse through text files a page at a time.

Package Classification

As of Debian 2.1, the distribution includes over 2000 packages. To help make some sense out of the complete Debian list, the packages are categorized according to purpose. Package-browsing tools can normally be configured to sort packages according to their section (see Figure 7.1).

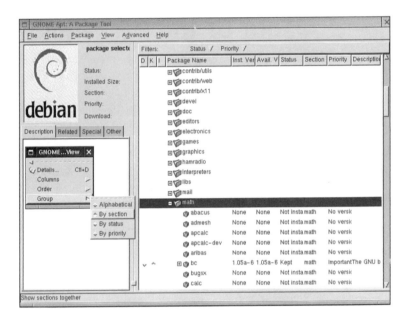

Figure 7.1

Distribution sections in gnome-apt. dselect also groups packages by section, albeit in a less graphical manner.

Currently, the standard distribution sections are as follows:

- **admin**—Tools that assist in system configuration.
- **base**—Packages that make up the core of a GNU/Linux system. Most of the packages from this section are automatically installed as part of the Debian base system.
- **comm**—Communications tools that *aren't* Internet-related. For instance, software for sending and receiving fax documents is found in this section.
- **devel**—Programming tools.
- **doc**—Manuals and other documentation.
- **editors**—Editor packages, mainly for plain text.

- **electronics**—Packages primarily of interest to electronic engineers.
- **games**—A selection of entertainment programs.
- **graphics**—Applications for working with image files, plus some lower-level graphical tools.
- **hamradio**—Programs of special interest to radio amateurs.
- **interpreters**—Runtime code used to execute programs written in various interpreted languages. Some other packages depend on these, but programmers might also want to install them manually.
- **libs**—Libraries of shared code used by other programs. You usually won't need to install these manually—they are selected automatically by the dependency system when required.
- **math**—Programs for performing mathematical tasks.
- **misc**—Packages that don't fit anywhere else.
- **net**—General network-related software.
- **news**—The Internet news (discussion groups) system.
- **otherosfs**—Programs that assist compatibility with other operating systems and filesystems.
- **oldlibs**—Old versions of libraries, needed for compatibility with old binary programs.
- **shells**—Alternative command-line interpreter programs.
- **sound**—Tools for playing and recording sounds.
- **tex**—Packages related to the TeX and LaTeX document-preparation systems, described in the section "Text Formatting Languages."
- **text**—Text processing utilities, dictionaries, and so on.
- **utils**—Various smaller utilities.
- **web**—Browsers, servers, and other tools.
- **x11**—The X Window System.

Packages are also given a priority: Important, Required, Standard, Optional, or Extra. Packages in the first two categories are involved in the day-to-day running of your system, and many of them are working behind the scenes. Packages you install yourself to perform specific tasks are normally classified as one of the three lower priorities.

Text Editors

Plain text editors (as distinct from word processors) are among the most essential UNIX applications. At the very least, you will occasionally need a text editor to manage system configuration files. You might also want to use such a program for composing email messages, and possibly for writing programs. Most UNIX editors are very powerful tools once you are familiar with them. Some even go as far as to have their own built-in programming languages to help you customize their behavior.

There is a wide range of editors to choose from. vi and emacs are the most popular, but you might like to experiment with some of the others. Some of these editors run in a text environment, while others require the X Window System. You might prefer to use a windowed editor for normal use, but bear in mind that one day you may want to use your machine without an X server. Therefore, it is helpful to be familiar with an editor that runs on a text console.

- **GNU Emacs** is the official standard editor of the GNU project. It can be used at many levels—it is quick and easy for simply editing a configuration file, but it also has sophisticated support for programmers. If you know the LISP programming language, it is easy to add new functions to the application. Emacs is sometimes described as a *self-documenting* editor because it has a built-in documentation browser that can be accessed via the Help menu.

- **X Emacs** is the editor for those who didn't believe it was possible to add any more features to GNU Emacs. This is one of the clearest examples of an open source project that split in two. This version provides most of the same facilities as the GNU version, but adds a more graphical interface plus various other extensions, including its own Web browser.

- **joe** is a small text-console editor that is simple and easy to learn. It takes its inspiration from the old DOS WordStar program.

- **vi** has a long heritage, and is widely considered the standard editor for UNIX systems. vi implementations can be small, and are very powerful. But it isn't the easiest program to learn. vi users need to get used to switching between insert mode, used for typing text, and command mode, used for more sophisticated editing actions. In fact, the user-hostile reputation of UNIX might be attributed in some part to users who stumbled into vi and never could leave. For those who are interested, the answer is to press **Escape** to ensure you are in command mode, and then type **:q!** to quit without saving changes. Unlike modeless editors, vi commands are made from normal characters, rather than relying on modifier keys such as Control to identify keystrokes which are intended as commands.

  But many of those who *do* persevere soon become vi addicts and won't touch anything else. And it has the big advantage in that you will find a copy installed on virtually any UNIX-like machine you find. Today, there are a number of editors that answer to the name *vi*. Of those supplied with Debian, nvi is closest to the original editor. elvis and vim add additional features, and vim also has the option of a windowed interface with a simple menu system.

- **wily** is a interesting editor for the X Window System, and is worth investigating if you are looking for a simple but powerful programmer's editor. It has a mouse-driven user interface, and it is one of those X applications that really does need a three-button mouse—the three-button emulation mode of the X server isn't adequate.

Internet Applications

Once your Debian system is running and configured, the chances are good that you will soon want to use it to access Internet resources. If you have a direct connection, you can start using these programs straight away. If you are using a modem, Chapter 8, "Advanced Configuration," describes how to configure and use dial-up Internet connections.

Web Browsers

Currently, the main browser for most GNU/Linux users is Netscape 4 (see Figure 7.2). This browser is available in Navigator (standalone Web browser) and Communicator (integrated email and news clients) variants.

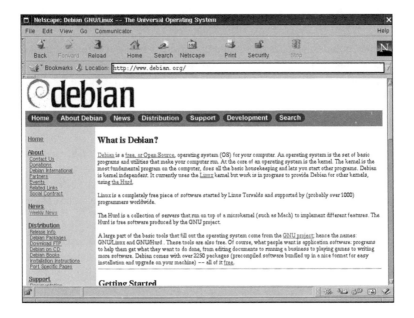

Figure 7.2

Netscape is the most popular Web browser for GNU/Linux. It looks the same as the Windows and MacOS versions.

Debian splits the Netscape Communicator application into several packages. Select either `communicator-base` or `navigator-base` depending on whether you are interested in using the messaging components. There are also optional packages such as `netscape-java`, which includes the runtime support for Java applets. In some versions you may find separate static and dynamic versions. The dynamic version is smaller, but it requires that you have proprietary Motif library files installed.

When you install the Debian Netscape packages, the browser program itself is launched via a Debian-specific script. This does not allow the root account to run the browser. There is a valid security concern behind this restriction: Web browsers can run Java and JavaScript code downloaded from the Internet, and it is possible that a copy of Netscape running with root privileges could allow unauthorized modifications to system files. In any case, there is really no reason why you should *want* to run a browser using the root account: All everyday computing should be done using a normal user account.

Netscape Navigator is a fairly old program now, and compliance with the latest Web standards is rather patchy. In 1998, Netscape made the surprise move of releasing the source code of its browser packages. Since then, development of a new version of the browser (which has, in fact, become a complete rewrite) has been carried out cooperatively by Netscape employees and community developers. The resulting browser promises to be among the most standards-compliant ever written. The home page for this open development effort can be found at `http://www.mozilla.org`.

The Web site includes regular status updates and links to development snapshot versions. Even if you aren't a programmer, you can help browser development by running these snapshots and writing up reports of any bugs you find. Once a Mozilla browser is ready for release, it is likely to replace Netscape 4 as the standard browser for Debian users.

There are various other browsers you can use. In particular, `lynx` is a browser with a difference: It runs on a text console (or in a terminal window under X, of course). This sounds a little strange to people used to graphical browsers, but for well-designed Web sites, it can be surprisingly usable. And because it doesn't need to download image files, using `lynx` could actually speed up your browsing. It is a standard Debian package, and quite small, so you might like to give it a try.

One final Web-related tool worth knowing about is the `wget` package. This is not a browser but a simple command-line tool that allows you to download a file from any Web URL (HTTP or FTP). It also has modes that allow you do download whole Web sites—helpful if you have a dial-up connection and want to keep a copy of some Web pages for reference.

Electronic Mail Clients

The Internet electronic mail system was developed largely by UNIX users, so it is not surprising that there is a good selection of powerful clients available to Debian users. They can be split broadly into two groups: text-based clients that can be run on a text console or in an `xterm` window, and graphical systems that require the X Window System. Today, the graphical solutions are becoming more popular, but these aren't necessarily the best answer—the text-based programs have been developed over many years and work extremely well.

Regardless of the mail client you are using, it will normally read messages from your system INBOX file, which is located in the `/var/spool/mail` directory. Where your other mail folders—old messages, archives of sent messages, and so on—are stored depends on the program you use. Most popular clients use the same format for mail folders, but the directory where they are stored will vary. So it's worth finding one mail client that you like and sticking to it.

One of the most popular graphical programs is the Messenger mail client built into the Netscape Communicator Web browser (see Figure 7.3). To set this up, open the Preferences dialog box from the Netscape Edit menu and adjust the Mail and News preferences to suit your system.

The most important options are those in the Mail servers section. To read messages from your normal system inbox, you should set your incoming mail server to Movemail. If you have a permanent network connection and your administrator has told you to use a specific outgoing mail server, you can enter details of that in this section, too.

But if you are using a dial-up network connection, or don't know about any outgoing mail server, you want to use your own machine as a mail server. Set the SMTP server option to localhost, and then make sure that you have the exim mail transport package installed and configured properly (see Chapter 8 for more details).

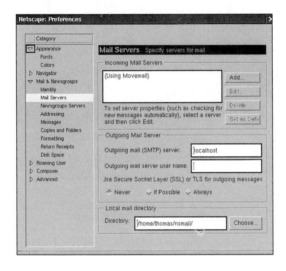

Figure 7.3

Netscape Communicator offers an easy-to-use graphical mail system.

Other graphical mail clients that you might like to look at include KMail (from the KDE project) and tkrat.

The standard text-based client for Debian is elm, an old favorite of many UNIX users. But it faces stiff competition from mutt (see Figure 7.4), a highly configurable program that arguably has better support for MIME, the standard used to encode files attached to email messages. Although mutt may not be as graphically appealing as some of the windowed solutions, it competes well on features and performance.

While most of the graphical mail clients include simple built-in editors, elm and mutt adopt the simpler solution of running a separate program for composing messages. They normally default to using vi as the primary editor. If you want to change this editor, you should set the EDITOR environment variable.

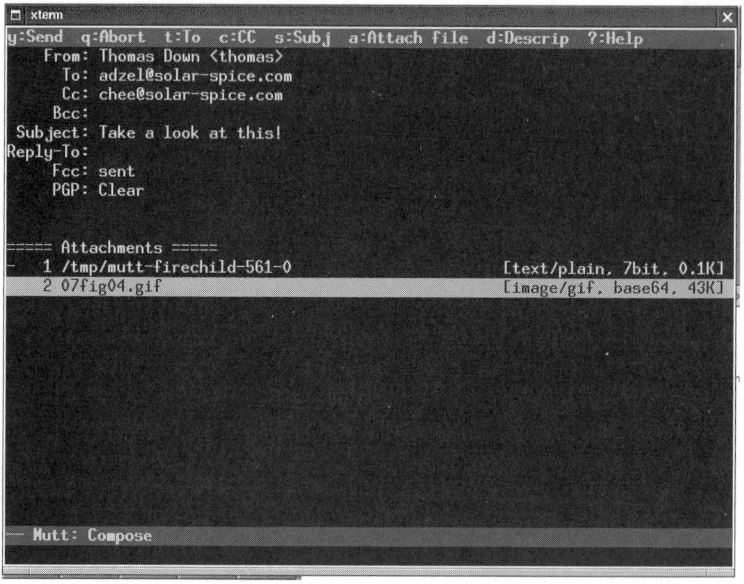

Figure 7.4

Mutt is a fast, flexible email client that runs on a text console.

CHOOSING YOUR ENVIRONMENT

Some UNIX programs can be configured using parameters called *environment variables*. Every program on the system has its own list of variables, and these are passed on to child programs. So if you have two text-console sessions running in separate `xterm` windows and you set an environment variable in window 1, it will affect all programs you run in window 1, but not those started from window 2. You can see the current set of environment variables at any time by typing `env`.

Environment variables can be set using a command in the form

```
export <variable>=<value>
```

For instance, to set the **EDITOR** variable, which many applications use as a hint for the name of a text editor program they can use, you type

```
export EDITOR=emacs
```

In practice, you will probably want to make this setting permanent. If you are using the X Window System, you can add the command to your `.xsession` file, thus ensuring that it runs every time you start an X session. The variable setting will then be passed on to every program you run within that X session. If you set environment variables in the .xsession file, you should put the command near the top of the file, before you run any programs.

If, on the other hand, you normally log on using a text console, set the environment variables in a different configuration file: .profile.

Productivity Applications

When GNU/Linux first started to emerge as a major player, one of the main criticisms of it was the lack of basic productivity applications such as word processors and spreadsheets. This argument is sometimes heard today, even though it is no longer true—there are a number of solutions available, both free and proprietary.

Word Processing

Currently, the most feature-rich word processors are commercial offerings such as Corel WordPerfect. This is free for non-commercial use. If you are interested, look at Corel's Linux support site at http://linux.corel.com.

Modem users beware though—it's a large file to download. Incidentally, Corel has also been talking about Linux releases of many of its other applications.

One of the most promising open source offerings is AbiWord (see Figure 7.5). Development of this package is coordinated by a company, AbiSource, which offers it for sale commercially. You can order a CD-ROM from the Web site. But development is entirely open, with much of the code contributed by external developers. It is released under a free license, the GNU GPL.

It has been designed with portability in mind, with development taking place in parallel on UNIX, Windows, MacOS, and BeOS. The UNIX version uses the GTK user interface toolkit, making it look rather like the GNOME applications (although it isn't directly connected to that project). AbiWord doesn't provide the same range of features as the latest commercial word processors, but it does offer a clean, friendly interface, and development is progressing rapidly. Project news, and up-to-date Debian packages, are available from http://www.abisource.com.

There are a number of other open source alternatives you might like to look at. The KOffice project (related to the KDE desktop environment) provides KWord and the GNOME developers are working on their own word processor, gwp.

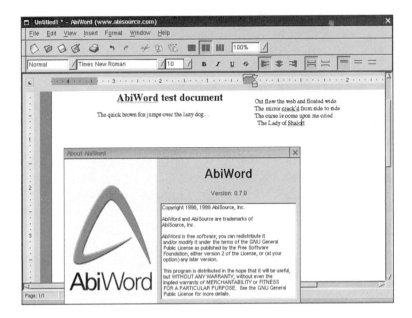

Figure 7.5

AbiWord is an open source word processor that's gaining a strong following.

Text Formatting Languages

While most people now prefer to use word processors that follow the "what you see is what you get" (WYSIWYG) model, there is an alternative approach to document production that remains quite popular in UNIX communities: Write your document as a plain text file, with formatting commands, and then run it through a separate program to produce the final, formatted version.

These systems have steeper learning curves than WYSIWYG packages. But once you are familiar with the basic commands, producing professional-looking documents is easy, and can be quicker than trawling though complex menu structures for the option you want.

Text formatting languages are very useful for producing documents that fit into a well-defined structure—scientific reports, for instance. Both the systems mentioned here provide powerful methods for handling cross-references between sections of a large document, and for automatically generating bibliography sections.

The best known document formatting language is LaTeX, which is actually an extra layer of code that extends the features of an older system called TeX. This has been a popular tool for producing scientific and mathematical texts for many years. Debian includes the tetex system, which includes LaTeX and many related packages. These are all found in the **tex** section of the package listing. As a minimum, you will want the tetex-base and tetex-bin packages installed. There are also packages of documentation, and a number of books about LaTeX are available. You may also be interested in lyx, a windowed word processing program which uses TeX to format the finished documents.

An alternative system, which provides similar functionality and a simpler design, is the curiously named Lout system. This includes many features provided by LaTeX extension packages as standard, and compiles documents directly to Postscript files, which are easy to view and print on a Debian system. It is easy to set up—just install the lout package, plus tools for viewing and printing Postscript files, and go. The lout-doc package contains a comprehensive manual (written in Lout, naturally).

If you are using one of these text formatting languages, you will almost certainly want to install ghostscript and integrate it into your printing system as described in Chapter 6, "The First Steps in Debian." You should also look at the gv package, a convenient ghostscript frontend that allows you to preview Postscript files onscreen.

Spreadsheets

Spreadsheets are another of the office-type applications that have been relatively slow in appearing on Linux systems. But both the GNOME and KOffice projects now have promising spreadsheets. The GNOME solution, included in recent Debian releases, goes by the name of gnumeric (see Figure 7.6).

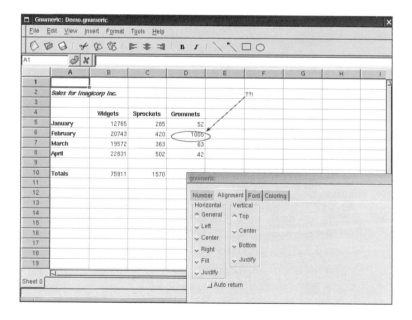

Figure 7.6

The Gnumeric spreadsheet has a familiar user interface.

Graphics Packages

For UNIX users looking for a painting and photo-retouch package, there is one obvious choice—the Gimp (GNU Image Manipulation Program). Ever since its release, this has been a showcase program for the free software movement. It offers a huge range of functionality, all accessible from a polished user interface (see Figure 7.7). It stands up well against proprietary competitors running under Windows or MacOS, and offers some interesting features of its own, such as a built-in programming language that allows expert users to automate complex sequences of operations.

Figure 7.7

The Gimp offers all the standard painting and photo-retouch features.

The other major class of graphics application consists of vector graphics packages, often used for technical drawings and illustration. There isn't (yet) a UNIX vector graphics package that compares to the Gimp. But the sketch package, distributed with Debian, is looking very promising (see Figure 7.8).

Others that are worth looking at include KIllustrator (from the KOffice project) and GYVE. These aren't currently included in Debian, but you will find announcements of the latest releases of these on Freshmeat.

Graphics-manipulation is a complex topic, and there are many other packages that you might find of interest. If you want to try your hand at 3D modeling, the blender package is worth a try. There are also a number of packages, such as gnuplot, that you might find helpful when generating graphs in scientific and mathematical documents.

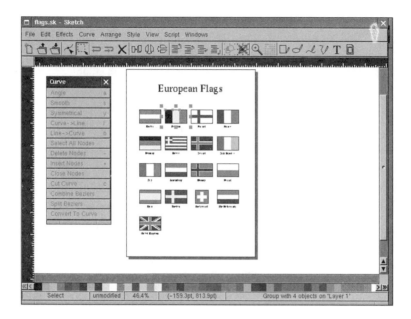

Figure 7.8

sketch may be the package you are looking for if you want an illustration tool.

Internet Services

GNU/Linux systems are eminently suitable for use as server machines, either on the Internet or in an Intranet environment. There are all kinds of network services available as standard Debian packages. The most popular ones are listed here.

- **Apache** is the server program that drives more than half of all sites on the World Wide Web. The default configuration should work well if you just want to use your machine to serve a few personal Web pages, but there are many configuration options to consider if you are setting up a serious installation. After installing the package, you can test your new server and read the manual at the same time by running the Web browser and looking at http://localhost/.
- **exim** is the standard Internet mail transport server for Debian systems. It is the one Internet server that most users will want to keep installed—it is useful even if you never use any kind of Internet connection. Exim configuration is described in some detail in Chapter 8.
- **IMAP** servers, such as those included in the Debian imap package, allow users on remote computers to access mailbox files stored on your machine. This is what you want if you are setting up a single mail server machine for an office or home network. If you are interested in client/server mail systems, look at the IMAP home page, http://www.imap.org.

- **samba** takes its name from the *server message block* (SMB) protocol family, which provides the facilities commonly referred to as Windows networking. This package allows a GNU/Linux machine to offer file and print server facilities to Windows clients. Information on the package is available from http://www.samba.org.

Now a few words of warning: Whenever you run an Internet server, you are opening a potential security hole on your system. There are two ways in which Internet server programs can enable security violations:

- First, bugs in the server code can give attackers the chance to make the server process behave in unexpected ways—which can sometimes include executing arbitrary commands on your system!
- Secondly, even a totally bug-free server program can sometimes violate system security if it isn't correctly configured. For instance, a Web server may be offering directories of files to the outside world without your knowledge.

There is no simple answer to keeping your computer secure, other than unplugging it from the network. But as a Debian user, you can do a lot to protect yourself from server bugs simply by keeping all packages on your system up-to-date, and regularly checking the Debian home page to make sure there aren't any security alerts relating to server packages you use.

Configuration errors are a little harder to avoid. Most server packages supplied with Debian have relatively safe default configurations. (If you see a package that you think has bad defaults, consider getting in touch with the package maintainer and suggesting an alternative.)

But even so, whenever you install a server, you should immediately read the documentation and then check through the configuration files yourself. And don't run servers unless you have to. Before you install a new one, be certain that you really do need it, and that you will have time to keep the configuration up-to-date. If you experiment with a server and then decide you don't want it, remove the package immediately.

Finally, if you have a permanent connection to the Internet as a whole, but are only running servers for the benefit of a small group of users (who will probably be using the local network), consider protecting your machine by configuring a *firewall* in the network subsystem. Firewalling gives you complete control over which computers are allowed to connect to your machine. If you are interested in this option, the IPCHAINS HOWTO document is a good place to start.

Programming Tools

UNIX systems have always been popular with programmers. It is not surprising, therefore, that there is a wide variety of free programming tools that you can use on a Debian system. If you are an experienced programmer, you will almost certainly find what you are looking for. If you want to learn a new programming language, using Debian tools can be a big advantage—you will be able to experiment with professional tools without paying for expensive proprietary products.

Some programming tools can also be important even if you never intend to write a line of code yourself. While these days the majority of popular Linux software can be found in binary format (at least for Intel platforms), more obscure pieces of code may still be easier to obtain in source format.

Building your own binaries is normally quite easy (see Chapter 5, "Making Your Selection"), but you will need development tools. Finally, you might want to recompile the Linux kernel itself (see Appendix A, "Kernel Management," for instructions and some circumstances under which you might wish to do this). If so, you need some basic tools.

The C Compiler

The early development of the UNIX operating system and the C language were closely linked. It is not surprising then that C is still the primary language for UNIX and Linux development. The standard C compiler for Linux-based systems is GCC, the GNU C compiler. Over the years, this compiler has gained support for a number of other languages: C++, Objective C, FORTRAN, and Pascal, with more on the way. Recently, its name has been changed to *GNU Compiler Collection* (still GCC).

The current versions of GCC are a little confusing. After the release of GCC 2.7, development work branched, and effort went into the development of the EGCS (experimental GNU compiler system) package. EGCS features better performance and support for more programming languages. Once this was established, development of the old GCC slowed dramatically. Debian 2.2 is likely to be released with EGCS as the main C compiler. But recently, the projects have re-merged, and the programs currently under development using the EGCS name will eventually become GCC release 3. You can read the latest news about GCC development yourself at http://gcc.gnu.org.

Fortunately, whether the distribution you are using is supplied with GCC or EGCS is normally not too important. Even if you are using an EGCS compiler, it will still be called gcc! As a minimum, install the gcc package. This is the core of the system, and allows you to compile C programs. You might then want to add g++ if you use C++, gobjc for Objective C support, g77 for FORTRAN 77, and gpc for Pascal.

Code Libraries and Headers

Debian includes many libraries of shared program functions that can be used by many programs. These libraries provide a wide range of services, from basic mathematical operations to specialist services, such as the libjpeg library for programs that need to manipulate JPEG-format images. The library packages are selected automatically when you install a program that requires them. But if you want to compile a program that requires one of these libraries, you need some extra files from the developers package. These extra files have names like libjpeg-dev.

If you are compiling a modern open source application, it will probably come with an automatic configuration script that scans the system for libraries it requires. If a library is reported as missing, make sure that the relevant developers' package is installed.

Debian, in common with most UNIX-like systems, includes one rather special library, called the *standard C library* (libc). As the name suggests, this library is used by all programs written in the C language. It also serves as the most important layer of insulation between a normal application program and the Linux kernel. Even some programs written in languages other than C rely on at least some of libc's functionality. As a result, the libc implementation is one of the most important packages on your Debian system.

Traditionally, Linux-based operating systems have used the Linux libc implementation. This version evolved from an early version of GNU libc. Linux libc went through various versions in the early days of Linux, but the only version you come across today is version 5.

Developers from the GNU project were also working on their libc implementation (glibc). With the release of glibc 2.0, this implementation was considered superior to the old Linux libc. So recent Linux distributions, including Debian releases since 2.0, have included glibc. Just to be confusing, when glibc 2 is installed on a Linux-based system (it works with various other kernels, too), it is sometimes also called libc6. Indeed, the main Debian package containing the library is called libc6.

For normal users, the differences between the two libc implementations are not too important but, from a programmer's perspective, the libraries are not entirely compatible. In particular, there is no binary compatibility: Software that was compiled for one library will not run with the other. All the applications in a recent Debian system are compiled for glibc 2, but you might still find the occasional program that is only available in binary format for libc5 systems. In recognition of this fact, Debian still ships a libc5 package in the oldlibs section. This should get any old applications you need to use up and running.

In addition to application packages, other library packages also depend on libc. This generally shouldn't be an issue for most people, but the package-naming system still contains some relics of the library switch-over.

Whenever libraries were converted to work with glibc 2, a *g* was added to the name. For instance, the xlib6 package (which contains the fundamental library for all X Window System clients) became xlib6g. Non-g versions of some of the key libraries can still be found in the oldlibs section. For general use, the rule is that if a g version of a library package exists, use that. But note that for library packages added since the libc switch-over, there will probably only be a glibc 2 version, without the g.

Debian release 2.2 includes a slightly updated C library, glibc 2.1. This is a less dramatic change, and shouldn't cause any problems for most users. Moreover, the glibc developers have added mechanisms in version 2.1 so that applications compiled to work with this version will be compatible with *all* future releases, no matter what changes are made.

Interpreted Languages

There are a number of powerful interpreted languages popular with UNIX users, especially for writing small, one shot programs. If you are looking for a simple scripting language, consider the `perl`, `python`, and `tcl` packages. Perl, in particular, is well known as a popular language for writing *CGI scripts* (programs that produce dynamic content for the Web). A simple Web search should turn up plenty of example Perl CGI programs. But if you don't like the look of the Perl code, the other two packages can perform similar tasks very well, too. You should find tutorial books on all three of these languages in any good computing bookstore.

Even if you haven't programmed before, consider looking at one of these languages. They are all good for writing simple programs for automating everyday tasks, and it's remarkable what you can achieve in just a few lines. On their own, or in combination with a text formatting language, you can use any of these systems to perform many of the functions you normally associate with macro languages in office-type application suites.

Other Programming Tools

The primary tool of every programmer is the text editor. Most common UNIX editors are designed with the needs of programmers in mind, and some (especially the Emacs variants) can interact with other programming tools to act as complete integrated development environments.

There is also a wide range of other tools that most programmers use. For example, `make` automates the compilation process, and you will certainly need it if you are going to build any major packages from source. If you are thinking of actively taking part in major open source projects, you may need the `cvs` version-management tool in order to fetch the latest versions of the source code from the developer's central repository. Finally, you might want to look at the `gdb` debugger, plus a wide range of smaller programming tools available under the devel section of the Debian package listing.

Java

Although the Java language isn't as dominant as some people suggested it might become, a fair amount of software is now written in this language. Java applications run on any platform, but you need a suitable runtime system installed in order to use them. There are two types of Java software that you might encounter: Applets and applications. *Applets* are small programs embedded in Web pages, and the Linux Netscape packages handle these programs fine.

There are also some standalone Java applications around. The normal way to run these standalone applications under Debian is to use the *Blackdown* port of Sun's Java Development Kit (JDK), which is included as a Debian package in the non-free section. As the name suggests, this contains not only the files needed to run Java applications, but also the standard Java compiler plus other tools for programmers.

There are also several open source alternatives to the proprietary Sun JDK. You might like to try the `kaffe` package, also included in Debian. And a new system, Japhar, is currently under development.

Summary

This chapter listed a selection of the most important Debian packages. The packages listed here should offer solutions to many common computing tasks. If you want something else, take a browse through the main package listings in `dselect`, or try a web search.

Having taken a look at some of the application software available, the following chapters return to the subject of configuring the core components of a Debian system.

CHAPTER 8

Advanced Configuration

This chapter covers some of the more advanced configuration mechanisms for your Debian installation. First, it considers the init system, responsible for setting up the system immediately after booting. It also contains instructions for configuring two of the most important subsystems of a Debian installation: dial-up networking and the email transport system. Finally, it revisits the mount command and considers methods for managing UNIX file systems. By the time you have finished this chapter, you should be able to configure a Debian workstation for use in a wide variety of situations.

If you are still looking for more information, especially about setting up a Debian-based server machine, the Linux Documentation Project HOWTOs can be a good place to start. There are also a number of books available, covering both general UNIX administration and specific subjects such as networking. Finally, Chapter 11, "And Finally—Welcome to the Community," describes some of the most important Internet resources provided by the Linux community. There may be a Web site that answers your question or, failing that, a mailing list where you can ask the experts.

The Initialization Scripts

When you boot a Debian machine, the first thing you see is a number of messages produced by the kernel as it starts up. But then a second phase of the boot process begins. The kernel runs a special program called init, which is responsible for setting up the system so it's ready for use. This includes mounting any disk partitions you use and initializing the networking system.

The init system also starts a number of background processes that are required for the normal operation of a UNIX system. These are historically called *daemons*, a contraction of *disk access monitors.* In modern UNIX-like systems, daemons perform many functions, ranging from Internet services to the scheduling of regular system-housekeeping jobs.

For reference, the init program used by Debian is modeled on the System V UNIX systems. A similar arrangement is used by a number of other Linux distributions, albeit often with a slightly different structure of configuration files. BSD UNIX systems use a different init design, and this has also been adopted by several less common Linux distributions.

Debian's init system is based around the concept of a *subsystem*—a specific part of the operating system that can be started and stopped more-or-less independently of the rest. A typical example might be a Web server program, which is normally started at boot time and continues running until the machine shuts down. But there is no reason why the Web server couldn't be stopped or started at any other time. You might, for instance, want to restart it in order to force it to re-read its configuration files.

There are also some lower level subsystems; for instance, starting the `mountall` subsystem causes the machine to mount any disk partitions you configured during the install procedure (excluding the root partition, which is automatically mounted when the kernel boots). A subsystem is defined by a simple program, normally written in UNIX shell script language (see the manual page for bash, the standard shell on GNU/Linux systems). These programs are stored in the directory `/etc/init.d`. You can run these programs yourself (as root) to manually start, stop, or restart the subsystem. For instance, this command

`/etc/init.d/cron stop`

will stop the cron daemon, a background process that allows users to schedule processes to run at specific times. This is the program that runs housekeeping tasks such as regular truncation of the system log files. Note that the file `/etc/init.d/cron` isn't the cron program itself—it is just a small script that can start and stop cron. If you install a Debian package that you want to start automatically at boot time, it will probably include its own subsystem script.

NOTE

If you ever want to write your own subsystem script (useful if you have a non-Debian program that you want to run as a standard background job), the file `/etc/init.d/skeleton` is a good starting point.

When init starts, it doesn't automatically start every subsystem defined in `/etc/init.d`. Instead, it only runs subsystems appropriate for a particular run level. Run levels are represented by a number, normally between 1 and 5, and you can specify that the machine boot to a particular level by entering a number at the LILO `boot:` prompt. Debian init defaults to run level 2 (this option, plus various other init configuration options, is defined in `/etc/inittab`). For most users, run level 2 is sufficient.

Occasionally, it may be useful to define some alternative configuration for the machine. For instance, if you have configured an X Window System display manager as described in Chapter 6, "The First Steps in Debian," you might like to configure an extra run level without the X Window System, so you still have the option of starting the machine in simple text console mode.

Another case occurs when you have a computer that is sometimes attached to a network, but that may also be used as a standalone workstation. In this case, you may choose to set up an alternative run level (level 3, for instance) so that any network servers that you normally use are not started. If you use network file systems (see Chapter 10, "Exploring the X Window System"), you will also want to ensure that the /etc/init.d/mountnfs.sh script is not started in the standalone run level. If you occasionally use a specialist network server (a database server such as mysql, for instance), you might want to create an extra run level to run this server.

The subsystems that should be started in a particular run level are defined by the contents of a directory called /etc/rc<number>.d. For instance, /etc/rc2.d defines the default run level. A run level directory contains symbolic links to some or all of the scripts in /etc/init.d. The default run level directory might contain a link called S89cron, which points to the subsystem script for the cron daemon. The S indicates that the subsystem should be started in this run level. There is then traditionally a two-digit number that tells init when to start the subsystem. Low numbers represent critical subsystems, which must be started early in the boot process, while higher numbers normally represent server programs that can be started later in the boot sequence. To prevent cron from being started in a particular run level, you can just delete the link, as follows:

```
rm /etc/rc2.d/S89cron
```

Note that this command is just deleting a link to the subsystem file, not the subsystem itself. If, later on, you decide that you want to reinstate it, you must create a new link:

```
ln -s ../init.d/cron /etc/rc2.d/S89cron
```

Run level directories can also contain symbolic links with names beginning with K. These are ignored when the system reboots, but if you change the run level of a running system, subsystems specified by K links are stopped. The most common example of this occurs when you halt or reboot the machine using the shutdown command. What this really does is switch to the special run level 0 or 6, respectively. If you look in the appropriate run level directories, you will see that all the main subsystems are stopped, and then some final shutdown operations are performed.

It is also possible to switch a running system to a new run level using the telinit command, but this is useful only if you have manually set up one or more run levels with a different selection of subsystems.

SYMBOLIC LINKS

Along with regular files and directories, UNIX file systems can contain another kind of object, called a *symbolic link*. This is effectively a special file that contains the name of another file or directory. When a program accesses the symbolic link, it actually sees the linked file. You can read and write to a symbolic link just like a regular file. However, deleting the link just removes the link itself—the file it represents remains untouched.

Symbolic links (sometimes called *symlinks* or *soft links*) are created using the `ln -s` command. For instance

```
ln -s test/links/mylink ../realfile
```

This creates a link called `mylink` in the directory `test/links`. The link connects to the file `test/realfile`. The destination of a link can either be specified as an absolute path (starting with a `/`) or a path relative to the directory containing the link, as in this example. When you specify a relative path, `..` indicates the parent directory. Symbolic links are a very powerful UNIX feature, but be careful when creating them. It is, for instance, entirely possible to link to a parent directory, thus creating a potentially confusing circular reference.

You may occasionally hear about *hard links*. This is another mechanism whereby more than one filename can represent the same file. Hard links are important to the internal working of UNIX file systems, but you will not normally need to create them yourself.

There is one more run level that you may sometimes hear about: level S, commonly referred to as *single-user mode*. In this mode, none of the normal subsystems are started. Instead, once the kernel is up and running, the system simply runs a single root shell. It is not possible to log on as any other user. The normal way to enter single user mode is to boot the machine with the word `single` on the LILO command line, for instance

```
linux single
```

On a modern system, you will never want to use single-user mode for normal operation. It is, however, sometimes used by expert users for major administrative work—especially system recovery after serious corruption. If you are having trouble booting your Debian installation in one of the normal run levels (sometimes called *multiuser mode*), try a single-user boot in order to recover data.

Configuring a PPP Network Connection

If you have a direct connection to the Internet (usually via an office or academic network), you should already have set it up during the installation process. If not, the standard way to connect is to dial up to an Internet service provider (ISP) using a modem.

At the moment, there aren't that many ISPs that specifically advertise support for Linux users (although if you do find one, you should consider supporting it). But the PPP technology used for dial-up connections is sufficiently standardized. You should, therefore, be able to easily connect your machine to most ISPs.

Before you start, you should register with an ISP and make sure you know the following pieces of information:

- The name of your account
- Your dial-up password
- The telephone number of your ISP's nearest access point

If available, it is also useful to know the IP address of the provider's DNS (domain name service) server. This address will consist of four numbers separated by periods. Later, you will also want the names of your ISP's mail server computers.

The first step toward connecting your machine is installing the ppp package, which allows you to establish PPP connections. You will also want the pppconfig package, which provides a simple method for configuring your connection. The pppconfig utility is a character-based interactive tool similar to the main Debian installation tool (see Figure 8.1).

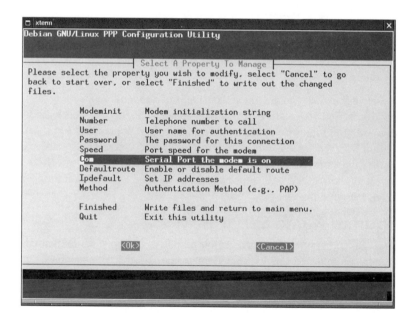

Figure 8.1

The pppconfig program sets up new dial-up network configurations.

The first time you run pppconfig you may be prompted for the IP address of a DNS server. If you don't know, enter `127.0.0.1` here, and then consult the next section, which describes the DNS system in more detail.

You will then have a chance to create an ISP information file. If you use only a single ISP account, accept the default name `provider`. But if you have several accounts or a single account with several different phone numbers, you should give each configuration you create a meaningful name. You will then be asked for the password and username of your ISP account. There are several methods offered for logging on to the ISP. Virtually every modern ISP supports the PPP method, so unless the documentation says otherwise, opt for that.

Next, you need to specify the serial device to which your modem is connected. The simplest case is an external modem. In this case, the device is `/dev/ttyS0` or `/dev/ttyS1`, which corresponds to the DOS devices COM1 and COM2, respectively. Internal modems, which usually appear as COM3 or COM4 under DOS, are `/dev/ttyS2` or `/dev/ttyS3`. But it is possible that you will have to use the `setserial` command to configure the serial driver correctly, as described in Chapter 2, "Getting Ready—Hardware." If you are unsure about the port on which your modem is installed, the wvdial package can normally detect it for you.

Most of the remaining options offered by the pppconfig program are for expert users, and the default values should be fine for any machine in which the PPP link is the main connection to the Internet. Finally, you can enter the phone number of the ISP's access point and specify whether to use pulse or tone dialing—modern phone networks generally use tones.

When you have finished, you are given the chance to check all your settings before saving them. If you find afterward that you have made a mistake, or you want to update the configuration, you have two choices. You can re-run pppconfig and create a new configuration with the same name as your old one. Or, if you are reasonably confident with text-based configuration files, you can manually edit the files in the `/etc/ppp/peers` directory. All the options used in PPP configuration files are described in the pppd manual page.

Configuring Name Services

Before you can use your dial-up connection properly, you need some method of connecting your computer to the Internet domain name service, a database that maps Internet hostnames to the numerical IP addresses used for low level network communications. The simplest solution is just to find the IP address of a DNS server machine provided by your ISP. You can configure your computer to use this by editing `/etc/resolv.conf` to include a line such as

`nameserver 243.1.32.180`

obviously substituting the IP address (four numbers) of your DNS server. Some ISPs offer two DNS servers, in which case you can add a second `nameserver` line. The second server is used automatically if the first one fails.

If you can't find a suitable DNS server address, you have another option: Make your Debian system an independent part of the DNS network. This is also a sensible option when you have accounts with several different ISPs and switch regularly between them. To make the Debian system a part of the DNS network, you need to install the standard nameserver package, bind, and then make your machine refer to itself for DNS resolution. For example

```
nameserver 127.0.0.1
```

NOTE

127.0.0.1 is a special IP address that always refers to the local host.

The bind program has its own subsystem script and will normally start automatically when the system boots. This can, however, cause some problems. If a program performs a DNS lookup when the machine is not connected to the Internet, it can hang for several minutes before realizing that the DNS system isn't going to respond. The Netscape Web browser is a particularly bad offender. The solution is to run bind only when the PPP connection is active.

First, remove the bind symbolic link from /etc/rc2.d (and the run-level directory for any other levels that you regularly use). Now look at the directory /etc/ppp/ip-up. All executable files in this directory are run, in alphabetical order, when a PPP connection is activated. You can start bind using a simple shell script program. For example

```
#! /bin/sh
/etc/init.d/bind start
```

There may be other scripts already present in the ip-up directory that expect a working DNS system—for instance, there will usually be a file that starts the delivery of any outgoing email messages. To ensure that bind is started first, you should give your script a name such as 00bind. You should then mark it as a program file by setting the *execute* access mode on the file:

```
chmod +x /etc/ppp/ip-up/00bind
```

To stop bind again when you deactivate the connection, you should place a similar script in /etc/init.d/ip-down:

```
#! /bin/sh
/etc/init.d/bind stop
```

With these scripts in place, you should never need to worry about DNS again.

Activating the Connection

Once you have your configuration file set up, you can activate the connection using the pon command. The general form to activate any configuration you have set up is as follows:

```
pon <provider_name>
```

If you set up a configuration using the default name, provider, activate it by issuing the pon command without any additional arguments.

If your modem has an audio-monitoring facility, you will hear it dialing and connecting. There is then a delay of a few seconds while the PPP systems at each end of the connection exchange details. Once this process is complete, your machine is fully connected to the Internet, and you can use network programs as usual. Try running a Web browser such as Netscape or Lynx to test the connection. If your ISP offers a Web cache server, you may want to configure your browser to use it. Most ISPs now offer a caching proxy server that stores copies of frequently accessed Web pages and can speed up your browsing. It is worth configuring your browser to take advantage of this service if it is available.

If there is a problem establishing the connection, error messages are written to the file /var/log/ppp.log. You can either view this file directly or use the plog command to view the last few lines added to the file.

By default, only the root account can activate connections. Once your PPP system is set up and working properly, you can allow normal users to activate connections by adding the users to the dip (dial-up Internet protocols) group. The easiest way to do this is using the adduser command, as follows:

```
adduser emily dip
```

When you have finished using a connection, just type **poff** to deactivate the PPP system and drop the connection.

Other Home Internet Solutions

The traditional alternative to standard dial-up connections for home and small office users is ISDN, a kind of digital phone line that offers faster dial-up connections. A number of ISDN cards are supported by recent Linux kernels—take a look at the isdn4linux FAQ, located at http://www.isdn4linux.de/.

In use, an ISDN connection is similar to a conventional dial-up link. You use the PPP protocol to establish a connection to your ISP (make sure that your provider supports ISDN—many do, but it is not universal in some areas) and, once configured, you will use the ISDN connection in the same way.

A newer solution is *digital subscriber loop* (xDSL) technology. This technology provides a permanent Internet connection, and setting up an xDSL connection is much more like setting up an Ethernet connection. Reports are that xDSL connections work fine with Linux systems, but many providers currently refuse to support Linux users. If you are interested, talk to your local providers, and then try a Web search—you may find some pages containing the personal experiences of local users.

Handling Electronic Mail

You have already seen a number of the GNU/Linux–compatible email clients (sometimes called Mail User Agents, or MUAs). But to use email, you also need another program—the *Mail Transfer Agent* (MTA). This program is responsible for filing each incoming message into the inbox of the appropriate user, and also for managing a queue of outgoing messages.

Internet email is sent using the Simple Mail Transfer Protocol (SMTP). This protocol defines how a program can connect to another machine on the network and transmit a message. The remote machine must be running an MTA, which accepts the incoming connection and stores the message.

In the simplest case, the message is addressed to a user on the computer that's receiving the message. In this case, the MTA program simply appends the message to the user's inbox file. But MTAs can also accept messages destined to users on other machines. When this happens, the remote MTA is effectively taking responsibility for the delivery of the message. In this way, some messages can be relayed from machine to machine around the Internet before eventually arriving at their destinations. You can trace the path taken by a message by setting your mail client to display all the header lines of the message. You will see a number of lines starting with the word `Received:`. Each of these lines represents a relaying step.

On a Debian system, the standard MTA is the exim program. Note that this is different from sendmail, the traditional UNIX MTA that is still used by many other Linux distributions. (The sendmail program is available as a Debian package but, unless you have special requirements, you will probably want to ignore it.)

Outgoing Mail

Even if you never connect your computer to the Internet, you should install the exim package. The exim package handles the simple case of email messages between users on the computer. Even if only one person is using the machine, there are some circumstances under which email can be automatically generated—for instance, if an error occurs during regular system-housekeeping tasks.

But most computers today have either a direct connection to the Internet or a dial-up modem link. There are two approaches that can be taken when handling outgoing messages:

- One solution is to attempt direct delivery of every message you send. In this case, the MTA inspects the part of the address that follows the @ character in the address and then connects to the appropriate machine.
- Alternatively, all messages can be passed directly to a dedicated machine called a *smart host*, which acts as a mail relay. If you are using a dial-up connection, your ISP will certainly offer a smart host—the documentation will probably describe it as *SMTP server* or *Outgoing mail server*. Commercial and academic networks usually offer a smart host as well; ask your network administrator for details.

Windows mail clients almost always rely on smart hosts for mail delivery. As a Debian user, you have a choice: exim is a fully featured MTA and is therefore capable of direct delivery. But smart hosts can offer a significant advantage when the receiving system is temporarily unavailable, because the smart host can keep trying to deliver the message at regular intervals.

If you don't have a smart host, your local copy of exim can keep retrying, too, but that isn't any help if you have a dial-up connection. And even if you have a permanent connection, you may want to switch off the computer or reboot the machine and use Windows instead, in which case any undelivered messages are waiting.

The exim program is configured by the file /etc/exim.conf. This is a rather complex file, but in most cases you can use an automatically generated default file. If you do decide you need to customize the system, the format of the configuration file is documented by files in the /usr/doc/exim directory. When you first install the exim package, the package installation scripts will run the eximconfig program to generate a standard configuration. If you make a mistake, you can re-run eximconfig at any time.

First, you are prompted to choose from several types of configurations. This is where you choose whether you are going to use a smart host. You are then asked a number of additional questions. You can accept the default values for many of these, but consider the following changes:

- The system's *mail name*. By default, UNIX mail clients usually generate messages with From: lines of the form <username>@<mail_name>. Most also give you the option to specify an alternative From: line. For instance, if all users on your machine are to have addresses like nick@solar-spice.com, you should enter solar-spice.com here.
- You are asked if you want to use the *Real-time Blackhole List* system to filter out junk messages. This option is relevant only when you are going to be using your Debian system to receive email directly, rather than using some other machine as an incoming mail server. If you are not receiving email directly, you should always answer "no" here.
- If you are using a smart host, you need to enter its name.
- Sometimes, messages relating to automatic system functions are sent to the root account. It isn't good policy to log on as root just to read these messages. For this reason, you have the chance to specify one (or more) normal user account to which root's mail should be redirected. You should always take advantage of this option.

Once you have set up a configuration file, you can use any standard UNIX mail tool to send messages. If you are using a dial-up connection, outgoing messages are held in a mail queue until you activate the connection, at which time they are sent. If you are logged on using the root account or any account that is a member of the mail group, you can check the contents of the mail queue using the mailq command. If you are using a dial-up connection and connect for very short periods of time, this option can be useful for ensuring that all messages have been sent.

Incoming Mail

If you have a permanent connection and your network administrator has allocated a name for your computer (such as adzel.solar-spice.com), it is possible to send email messages directly to any user account of the machine, for instance thomas@adzel.solar-spice.com. However, this can happen only when the computer is connected, switched on, and running Debian all the time. Some network administrators may ask you not to use this facility. Moreover, if you are using a dial-up network connection, this simply isn't an option.

The alternative is to allow a dedicated incoming mail server machine, normally operated by your ISP or network administrator, to receive mail on your behalf. Messages are stored there, and can be retrieved at any time using a special mail retrieval protocol. Mail servers operated by ISPs usually support the POP3 protocol for fetching messages, while corporate or academic servers may use an alternative system called IMAP. There are also some special mail systems, normally found in corporate environments, that rely on proprietary protocols—consult your network administrator if you think this might be the case.

If your mail is being stored on a POP3 or IMAP server, you want the fetchmail package. This package retrieves messages from the incoming mail server machine and then feeds them into your local mail system. You configure fetchmail by creating a text file in your home directory called .fetchmailrc. This file contains one or more lines listing the mail server accounts that the program should check for new messages.

If you have an ISP account with an email address of tdown@someisp.net, for example, you add the following line to your fetchmail configuration file:

```
poll mail.someisp.net protocol pop3 username tdown password
➥Bl3rdyBloop mda ""/usr/sbin/exim -bm thomas""
```

Each entry in a .fetchmailrc file *must* be a single line, so beware of editors that break long lines of text. Note that .fetchmailrc entries are designed to look like normal English sentences. This one specifies the mail server to check the username and password of an account there, and the name of a local account to which fetched messages should be delivered.

The mda (mail delivery agent) option specifies the command that should be used to inject the message into the normal mail system. This isn't actually the normal way of configuring fetchmail, but it bypasses some checks in the standard Debian mail system intended to prevent relaying of junk mail. These checks can also cause rejection of fetchmail messages and should therefore be avoided.

You might be surprised to note that the password is included in this file in plain text form. The fetchmail documentation explains in some detail why any attempt to hide the passwords simply leads to false security. The program does, however, check that your configuration file is not readable by other users. To make sure this is the case, remove the group and others readable and writeable access flags with a command such as

```
chmod og-rw .fetchmailrc
```

Once you have set up a .fetchmailrc file, you can fetch your messages by typing

```
fetchmail -a
```

This command includes progress reports as it downloads messages. If you are using a windowed environment, you will probably want to create an icon or menu item that acts as a shortcut for mail fetching.

Mail Filtering

By default, all messages that you receive are appended to your normal system inbox file. From there, you can read and manipulate them using a mail client of your choice. But if you receive very large volumes of mail—especially messages from high-volume Internet mailing lists—you might prefer to automatically filter out some types of message and store them in different mail folders. There are a number of standalone programs for filtering messages. The most popular one in the Linux community at large is procmail, which is available as a Debian package. But exim actually contains a very powerful filtering system of its own. This filtering system creates a file in your home directory called .forward. A very simple example is as follows:

```
# Exim filter
if $sender_address is ""nick@solar-spice.com"" then
  save $home/mail/nick
endif
```

This example filters out messages originating from one specific address and places them in their own mail folder. All other messages go into your system inbox as normal. But you are not restricted to just filtering messages on sender addresses—for all the options, consult the exim documentation.

Managing File Systems

When your Debian system starts up, it automatically mounts at least one, and possibly several, disk partitions. You can see the list of mounted partitions by typing **mount**. In addition to the partitions you set up during the installation process, you will see an extra file system mounted on /proc. This is a special file system: It does not represent any disk partition but instead allows normal programs to read certain pieces of data from the Linux kernel. For instance, when you use the ps command to obtain a list of running processes, it is actually reading data from files in the /proc directory.

As you saw in Chapter 3, "Getting Ready—Disk Space," you can easily mount additional file systems. Consider, for example, a Windows partition on /dev/hda1 (this is the normal location of your Windows C: drive on a dual boot Windows/Linux machine). To access this under Linux, first create a suitable mount point directory. For example

```
mkdir -p /v/win_c
```

The -p flag tells mkdir to create the /v directory as well, if it doesn't already exist. Then, use the mount command as follows:

```
mount /dev/hda1 /v/win_c
```

Note that in this example, `mount` doesn't need to be explicitly told about the type of file system to mount. It is always safe to specify the file system type using the `-t` option, but in most cases `mount` makes a reasonable guess.

Suppose, however, that you access that partition regularly. You can save yourself some typing by adding a line to the system configuration file `/etc/fstab` to automatically mount your DOS partition at boot time. A suitable line might be

```
/dev/hda1    /v/win-c   vfat    defaults   0    2
```

The `/etc/fstab` file has a column-based format. The first column specifies a device to be mounted. The second column is a mount point directory, which you should create yourself. Next comes the file system type to use—if in doubt, try mounting the file system manually as shown, and then type **mount** to find which type has been selected automatically. Alternatively, just use the `auto` option here, which allows the `mount` command to determine the type at mount time. The fourth column is a comma-separated list of special options to use when mounting this file system. When in doubt, start by choosing `defaults` here. The last two columns are optional and always have numerical values. They specify how various system-management programs should treat that partition and are described in the manual page for `fstab`. Values of 0 and 2 will suit most personal workstation setups.

It isn't always sensible to mount file systems at boot time, though. This is especially true in the case of removable media. On the other hand, it can be awkward to log on as root and execute a complicated `mount` command every time you need to access a device. Adding an entry to `/etc/fstab` can help in this case, too. For instance if you regularly use a CD-ROM device, you might like to use the following entry:

```
/dev/cdrom   /v/cdrom   iso9660   noauto,user,ro  0   2
```

If you installed Debian from CD, the installer will normally create a symbolic link from `/dev/cdrom` to your real CD-ROM device (for instance, `/dev/hdc`). If you didn't install from CD, you might want to create this link now. Virtually all CD-ROMs use the ISO 9660 file system type, so that option is specified here. But the most important part of this `/etc/fstab` entry is the `options` column. The `noauto` flag means that this device should not be mounted automatically at boot time, while the `user` flag means that it can be mounted by any user, not just root. Finally, `ro` is a hint that this is a read-only device—this option isn't strictly necessary, but it avoids encountering a warning message when you mount the device.

With an entry such as this, any user can mount a CD-ROM at any time by running `mount` with a single argument. For example

```
mount /v/cdrom
```

The graphical file managers supplied with GNOME and KDE provide methods for creating icons corresponding to mountable devices on your desktop. With a suitable

/etc/fstab entry and a properly set up file manager, a single click can mount a CD-ROM (or floppy disk or some other device) and open a window for viewing its contents.

An equivalent entry that allows users to mount floppy disks might look like this:

```
/dev/fd0  /v/floppy  vfat  noauto,user  0  2
```

There is no need for the ro flag in this case, since you will normally want to mount a floppy drive in read-write mode. But you can mark any partition as read-only if you like. This is sometimes useful when using hard disk partitions, which never need to be modified. Mounting hard disk partitions as read-only means they are less likely to become corrupted and may make access slightly faster.

Normally when you mount a file system, you specify a UNIX device name (either a hard disk partition or a floppy or CD-ROM drive) that contains file data. But this isn't necessary for all Linux file system types. You have already encountered the case of the proc file system, which provides access to kernel data structures rather than any physical device. This is mounted using an entry in the standard /etc/fstab file, and you will never need to modify this in normal operation. More interesting to the normal system administrator are special file systems that provide access to network file servers. These special file systems are covered in Chapter 9, "Life on a Network."

Summary

This chapter covered the configuration of some of the most important parts of a UNIX computer system: dial-up networking, electronic mail, and file system management. The theme of advanced configuration continues in the following two chapters. Chapter 9 contains more information on Debian's network support, with an emphasis on solutions that help to get the most out of a simple private network. Chapter 10 will help you to personalize a graphical user interface for your own uses.

CHAPTER 9

Life On a Network

The era of the computer as a standalone device is now past. Most offices are networked (and usually connected to the global Internet), while dial-up access is common for home users. Moreover, new technologies are making permanent Internet connections to the home increasingly practical, and many individuals with more than one computer are choosing to set up small private networks.

There are some big advantages to attaching your computer to a network. Even in a home environment, you can make your machines far more useful by sharing resources. As a Debian user, you already have access to a wide selection of powerful server technology. So if you have two computers, you can start experimenting with networks just for the price of a couple of Ethernet cards.

Private Network Addresses

First of all, you need to establish a few simple conventions for the names and IP addresses used in private networks. If you are connecting your machine to an existing network, ignore this section and set up your machine as the network administrator tells you. But if you are setting up your own network, *you* are the administrator, and you need to make certain decisions about the network.

Back in Chapter 4, "A Basic Installation," I suggested that if you were planning to connect your machine to a private network (that is, a network that isn't part of the Internet but that nevertheless uses the Internet protocol family), you should give it an IP address of the form 192.168.1.xxx. This form is a special reserved block of IP addresses that aren't normally used by computers connected to the Internet, but which are otherwise safe for general use.

Whenever you connect a new machine to your network, ensure that you allocate it a unique IP address. This doesn't apply just to Linux machines—any other computer can use the same network, so long as it has a unique address.

Next, you should allocate names for all computers on the network. On the Internet, the DNS (a sophisticated distributed database) is used to convert between computer names and IP addresses, but this is overkill for a simple private network. Instead, each machine on the network should have an /etc/hosts file that gives names to all the machines present. For instance, each of the three machines on my own network has an /etc/hosts file that looks like this:

```
# /etc/hosts for heatherdean.lan
# Thomas Down's personal network

127.0.0.1      localhost
192.168.1.1    firechild
192.168.1.10   adzel
192.168.1.11   sunspark
```

Note that the first entry is the special address, localhost, which always refers to the local machine. This is present in the default /etc/hosts on a newly installed Debian system and is important for system function. Don't delete it, or strange things could happen. Also note that each machine's /etc/hosts file contains an entry for itself as well as for the other machines on the network. If you have Windows systems on the network, they can also use a file to map between names and IP addresses. In this case, the Windows file is called C:\Windows\hosts.sam, but the file format is exactly the same.

Internet Servers

If your computer is attached to a network, you will probably want to run some network servers. These can perform any function from serving Web pages to allowing remote logins. Some Internet server programs—notably the Apache Web server—run permanently. This type of server is started by an init subsystem script, as described in Chapter 8, "Advanced Configuration." If you want to disable them, remove the relevant link from your run level directories, or just use the subsystem script to stop the server. Many servers, such as telnetd, the program that allows you to log on to a UNIX machine over a network connection, are run only when they are actually needed. There is a special *server of servers* called inetd that watches for incoming network connections and can start appropriate servers when required. Under Debian, inetd is started as part of the netbase subsystem. To change the behavior of inetd, edit /etc/inetd.conf, and then type

```
/etc/init.d/netbase restart
```

which kills and reloads the inetd daemon. If you have a permanent network connection, you should check through the list of services offered by inetd and comment out (disable) any you don't want by adding a # character to the start of the relevant line. If in doubt, when you are setting up a standalone workstation, it is normally safe to disable

ces in /etc/inetd.conf. The one important exception is the SMTP
important for the functioning of the computer's email system, even if
't have a permanent network connection.

n

een two ways to log on to a Debian system: via a text console or via
tem display manager. But you can also log on over a network. The
standard way to connect from one UNIX-type computer to another is using the telnet
command. For example

```
telnet adzel
```

If the remote machine is configured to accept remote logins (out-of-the-box Debian
installations normally are), you will see a new login prompt. Entering your username
and password will give you a shell prompt on the remote machine, and you can start
working as normal.

There are also Telnet clients for other types of computers. For instance, on a Windows
machine you can select Run from the Start menu, and then enter a telnet command.
The difference is that the Windows Telnet program runs in its own window and has to
emulate a UNIX text console in much the same way that xterm does when you run console programs under the X Window System. Unfortunately, it doesn't do this very well.
Simple command-line utilities run well, but I wouldn't recommend running a full-
screen program such as a text editor.

There are a number of alternative Windows Telnet programs available from shareware
software archives, and some of these have much better console emulations. Note also
that you find only the *client* side of the Telnet system on a Windows machine. These
systems normally don't support remote login themselves.

To allow remote logins, your computer must be running the server side of the Telnet
system using a program called telnetd (Telnet daemon). This program is started via
inetd, and you can disable it by commenting out a line in the /etc/inetd.conf file.

You might occasionally hear about rlogin, an alternative program that allows you to log
in to a UNIX system. Unlike Telnet, this allows trusted users to log in without entering
a password. Today, the ssh program, described in the section "Secure Remote Logins,"
offers a more powerful and secure alternative to rlogin.

Secure Remote Logins

The main alternative to simple Telnet is ssh (for *secure shell*). This is available as a
Debian package from the main non-U.S. server, plus its mirrors. The first benefit of ssh
is that the connection is encrypted: Even if your network is not secure, nobody can see
what you are typing (including your password). Moreover, if you are connecting to
another machine by ssh, you may not even need to use a password at all.

The ssh-keygen program generates a pair of authentication certificate files. You should
generate a pair for every account you use regularly. The private half of this pair of files

needs to be kept secure and should always be kept on the computer where it was originally generated. But the public section can be copied to your account on any other computer where ssh is installed. The private certificate allows you to securely authenticate yourself to any account that contains the public certificate. Thus, once you are logged on to one computer, you can safely access any of your other accounts without needing to type a password. If you use several different computers on a regular basis, this is a big advantage.

The ssh system also provides a variety of extra features over and above simple Telnet. In particular, if you are using the X Window System, you benefit from automatic, secure connection forwarding. This is explained in Chapter 10, "Exploring the X Window System," and can make running X applications across a network a lot easier.

There is also an scp program for securely copying files from one computer to another. If you want to use the ssh system, start by reading the manual pages for both the ssh client program and the sshd server.

Transferring Files

A traditional approach to exchanging files between UNIX machines is the FTP protocol. This is commonly used around the Internet—indeed, you may have obtained the Debian distribution via FTP. Standard Debian installations include an FTP server (ftpd) started via inetd. Using either the command-line ftp tool or various graphical programs, it is possible to log on to this FTP server (using your normal username and password) and store and retrieve files. It is also possible to configure an *anonymous* FTP server. In this case, remote users can access selected files by logging in using the name anonymous and giving their email address as a password. You will probably have encountered anonymous FTP while browsing the Web: URLs with the scheme ftp: specify files on anonymous FTP servers.

FTP can be a convenient method for transferring data between machines on a small network. But there are alternatives worth investigating. If you have the ssh system installed, you can just use the scp command to move files between machines. This command is designed to work similarly to the standard UNIX cp copy command, but when you enter the source and destination filenames, you can specify user and hostnames too, as follows:

```
scp thomas@adzel:projects/test/myfile test/myfile-local
```

The Network File System (NFS)

In previous chapters, you learned about the structure of the UNIX virtual file system, and how the mount command is used to access disk partitions. But when you mount a new file system, it doesn't necessarily have to come from a disk partition on the local machine. There are several systems that allow file systems to be mounted over a network. Once such a mount is established, you can have completely transparent access to files stored on another computer. There is a certain amount of work involved in setting up shared file systems, but if you find yourself transferring files between computers on a regular basis, this could be the simplest solution.

The classic UNIX file-sharing technology is the Network File System (NFS). NFS allows a server to export all or part of its virtual file system hierarchy. Suppose a server called adzel on your local network is exporting a directory called /usr/packages. With the Debian nfs-client package installed, you can mount this server with a command such as

```
mount -t nfs adzel:/usr/packages /v/adzel-packages
```

Once an NFS mount is established, you can access files within it just like local files. NFS is used primarily on local area networks in organizations with a large number of UNIX or Linux machines. There are also a few big-file servers on the Internet that can be NFS-mounted in read-only mode as a convenient alternative to accessing them by FTP.

As well as acting as an NFS client, your Debian system can export directories using the nfs-server package. But remember that, like any network service, there is a security risk associated with doing so. The case of exporting a directory to a single client machine is perhaps too easy, given all the potential administrative issues it opens up. Just add a line to /etc/exports, and then restart the /etc/init.d/nfs-server subsystem. For instance

```
/usr/packages      firechild(ro)
```

This means: Export the /usr/packages directory and allow read-only access to the machine named firechild. If you have more than two computers on your network, you can either list each machine individually or use various alternative notations to specify a group of machines. The details of the file format are described under "exports" in section 5 of the manual.

NFS is an extremely powerful technology. For instance, if you have several different machines and make equal use of all of them, you might want to keep your /home directory on just one machine and then NFS-mount /home on all the other machines on your network (you can list NFS mounts in /etc/fstab, just like in normal partitions).

NOTE

Accessing files over the network is normally slower than reading them directly from a modern hard disk, but the convenience of never having to explicitly transfer files from one machine to another can outweigh this factor.

There are some complications in administering an NFS system. If you are running anything other than a very simple setup, and especially if your NFS servers have permanent Internet connections, you should at the very least carefully read the NFS-HOWTO document, with an emphasis on the security sections. You might also want to read some books on professional UNIX network administration.

One of the biggest potential surprises for the new NFS user is that user and group information is transferred over the network in the form of numerical IDs rather than names.

So if the user IDs in /etc/passwd don't match the client and server machines, you may not be able to access your files. More distressing, you might even gain access to files belonging to a user who has been allocated the same ID.

For small networks with just a handful of users, the best approach is probably to manually check the /etc/passwd files on each machine and make sure that the UIDs match. When you create new accounts, you can force the use of specific IDs, as follows:

```
adduser —uid 2001 —gid 2203 thomas
```

For more complex installations, this becomes impractical. The obvious answer is to abandon the approach of keeping user information on each individual computer and instead move the information to a single central server. The best-known technology for achieving this centralization is the Network Information Service (NIS), a sophisticated system developed alongside NFS. Be aware, however, that installing this is itself a fairly serious undertaking. If you decide you do need to take this approach, look at the nis packages supplied with Debian, and carefully read the NIS-HOWTO document. Incidentally, it is not necessary to administer *all* accounts on a computer using NIS: You can use normal /etc/passwd entries as well. It's best to maintain normal /etc/passwd entries for at least the root account on each machine, so you can still log in if the NIS system fails.

Sharing Files with Windows Machines

As well as NFS, the Linux kernel can mount file systems exported over the network using the SMB protocol family. This is often called *Windows networking*, although UNIX servers running the Samba program can also act as SMB servers. To mount an SMB-shared file system, use a command such as

```
mount -t smb //winserver/c/directory /v/win-share
```

Note that, to fit in with conventions used in UNIX command-line interpreters, / characters are used in place of the \s used by Windows systems. If you have a mixed network with both UNIX and Windows computers attached, you might prefer to use SMB instead of NFS so that the same shared file systems can be used by all the machines on the network.

If all this sounds too complicated (and, like NFS, SMB networking can easily turn into something of an administrative headache once you have several computers and a number of users), a much simpler solution is to run an FTP server on your Debian machine. You can then use one of the many Windows FTP clients (a simple one is included with Windows itself) to fetch and store files.

Sharing a Printer

The standard UNIX lpr print spool manager includes the lpd daemon, a mechanism for sharing a printer between several machines. The first step is to set up the lpr system on the machine that's acting as the print server, as described in Chapter 6, "The First Steps in Debian." Once this is set up and tested, edit the file /etc/hosts.lpd, and list all the machines on the network that are allowed to print files on this server.

Now, on each machine that is going to be a printer client, install lpr, and add an `/etc/printcap` file similar to the following:

```
lp¦remote printer:\
     :lp=:\
     :rm=firechild:\
     :rp=lp:\
     :sd=/var/spool/lpd/lp:\
     :mx#0:\
     :sh:
```

Now create the corresponding print spool directory:

```
mkdir /var/spool/lpd/lp
```

and set the ownership and access mode:

```
chown lp.lp /var/spool/lpd/lp
chmod 0755 /var/spool/lpd/lp
```

This creates a local print queue called lp (which is the default queue used by the lpr command). All files placed in this queue are forwarded over the network and inserted into another queue (in this case also called lp) on a server machine called firechild. Note that there are no references to *magic filters* here—the print job is passed through any filters configured in the `/etc/printcap` file on the server machine.

Windows machines access shared printers using the SMB protocol. If you are running a Samba server to share files, you can also configure it to share a printer. Correspondingly, the smbclient package (one of the accessory packages for the Samba system) provides a simple tool that allows UNIX clients to print to a Windows shared printer.

Sharing an Internet Connection

Perhaps the ultimate in resource sharing for a home network is to allow all machines on the network to share a single Internet connection (probably a standard dial-up or ISDN line). The Linux kernel includes a function called *IP masquerading*, which provides an *almost* perfect method of doing this. The qualification *almost* is needed because machines connected using this method aren't normally able to accept incoming network connections; they can only establish outgoing connections. This is usually not a problem for most users. Indeed, it can avoid security problems, since users from outside your network cannot access any insecure network server programs that might be running. In recognition of this, installations of this kind are sometimes described as being *firewalled*.

For the rest of this section, it is assumed that you have set up all the machines on your private network as described earlier, with addresses in the 192.168.1.xxx range. One machine on the network should have a dial-up connection, with the PPP system set up as described in Chapter 8 (if not, make sure that this is working before you proceed). This computer is referred to as the *gateway* (see Figure 9.1). Note that, in a simple masquerading setup, the gateway is the only machine that needs to be running Linux. The remaining *client* machines can be running any operating system.

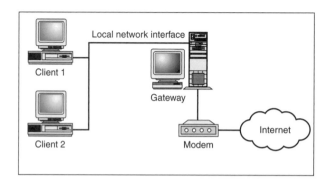

Figure 9.1

IP masquerading shares a single dial-up connection between all machines on a network.

So far, the chapter has considered only the case of a computer having a single IP address. But in fact, the gateway machine in Figure 9.1 has two: the *reserved* address, allocated by you and associated with the Ethernet interface, and another address, allocated automatically by your ISP and associated with the dial-up connection. When one of the client machines attempts to create an outgoing connection, the masquerading code on the gateway connects to the Internet proper on the client's behalf. Thus, outgoing connections from all the machines on the network appear to come from a single IP address: the one associated with the dial-up connection. This leads to the term *masquerading*.

The first step is to set up the client machines on the network. They need to know the IP address of the gateway machine. For Debian systems, this is specified by the GATEWAY=... line in /etc/init.d/network. Since the client machines will have access to the Internet, they will also want access to the domain name service. The easiest way to set this up is to run the bind program on the gateway, as described in Chapter 8, and then set all the clients to use the gateway as their name server.

Now, to actually provide the masquerading system, ensure that the ipfwadm package is installed on the gateway. Activate the dial-up connection, and then type (as root)

```
ipfwadm -F -p deny
ipfwadm -F -a masquerade -S 192.168.1.0/24 -D 0.0.0.0/0
```

The address 0.0.0.0/0 is a reference to the Internet as a whole. To test this, go to one of the client machines and try to establish an outgoing connection to an Internet site— just fetching a page in a Web browser is a good test. This test should work just as if you had a dial-up connection directly to the client machine.

Once you have tested the system, you will probably want to move the ipfwadm commands to some location where they are executed automatically. To do so, place a script in /etc/init.d, plus symbolic links from your run-level directories to ensure that it is executed when you boot the machine. In the simplest case, you could just write a script like this:

```
#! /bin/sh


ipfwadm -F -p deny
ipfwadm -F -a masquerade -S 192.168.1.0/24 -D 0.0.0.0/0
```

This can be executed at boot time by placing it in /etc/init.d, marking it as executable using the chmod command, and creating a suitable symbolic link from your normal run-level directory. Another sensible location for masquerade scripts would be the /etc/ppp/ip-up and /etc/ppp/ip-down directories, first described in Chapter 8.

Note that the IP masquerading system has been rewritten in the Linux 2.2 kernel, and the official mechanism for configuring the gateway is the ipchains program. There is a small wrapper program that emulates the old ipfwadm system, but if you want to take advantage of the more powerful ipchains program, take a look at the IPCHAINS-HOWTO document.

Security Issues (or The Paranoid Bit)

You probably already have noted a security theme running throughout this chapter (and, indeed, most of this book). Any machine with a (non-firewalled) permanent Internet connection should be considered a potential target. And even dial-up machines are sometimes targeted by crackers. Note that use of the term *hacker* to refer to someone trying to gain unauthorized access to a computer system is frowned upon in the Linux community. An earlier use of hacker is applied to anyone who programs computers in a creative manner. Indeed, most major GNU/Linux developers would quite happily label themselves as hackers.

There are two main kinds of attacks that can be launched against a computer. Denial of Service (DoS) attacks normally cause the machine to crash. Such attacks are irritating to users but not usually serious unless they are applied to critical server machines. Linux-based systems are normally extremely resistant to DoS attacks.

More serious are techniques that allow the attacker to execute an arbitrary piece of code on a machine. These usually exploit bugs (often quite trivial-looking ones) in Internet server daemons. Once an attacker has found a security hole of this kind, the attacker will often be able to obtain full root access to your machine. Systems attacked in this way are sometimes used as bases for distributing illegal copies of software and other desirable files, relaying junk email, or launching attacks on other computers.

You might think this section sounds excessively paranoid. But personal experience from a period when my machine was connected to a large academic network tells me that crackers certainly *do* exist. I observed several attempted attacks (foiled by ensuring that any server packages running on my machine were kept up to date) and heard about a number of computers that were successfully cracked. In one case, the intruders installed a network traffic snooping system that deciphered around 500 username-password pairs before it was discovered—an excellent reason for using ssh instead of Telnet whenever possible.

But before you let this potential risk persuade you that connecting your computer to any kind of network is a bad idea, remember that security *is* possible. A machine running a recent Linux kernel and no Internet servers (either from inetd or as a standalone daemon) is actually very safe. In practice, you probably will want to run a few servers (at least the exim mail server and maybe sshd). So long as you always make sure you are running the latest versions and regularly check the Debian home page for security alerts, you are probably safe. GNU/Linux server programs are under intense scrutiny from some very paranoid people; thus, problems are found quickly. If you are running servers on a public network, it's also worth glancing through your system log files (in the /var/log directory) to check for anything out of the ordinary. You might also like to look at security tools that check the integrity of your system. For instance, the trip-wire program can monitor key system files and warn you if there is any unauthorized modification.

Summary

In this chapter, you have seen a number of methods for sharing resources between computers on a network. Modern networks are simple to install. The tools and servers supplied with Debian can help you to make the most of a network. Further information about using the X Window System in a networked environment can be found in Chapter 10.

This chapter emphasized techniques that are suitable for managing small networks, as might be found in the home or in small offices. Debian servers could also be used in much larger network installations. Some advice on large-network administration can be found in HOWTO documents, but you may also want to consult specialist books.

CHAPTER 10

Exploring the X Window System

This chapter takes a more detailed look at some of the key properties of the X Window System, used by Debian programs to provide a graphical user interface. Chapter 6, "The First Steps in Debian," showed that the system could be divided into client and server programs, which can communicate over a network connection. This chapter explains some of the practical consequences of this division and also looks further at how your X desktop can be customized.

X on Display

So far, the book has concentrated primarily on the case of a standalone workstation running an X server plus a selection of X client applications. But when you start an X client, you can tell it to connect to any display. According to X conventions, a display name has three parts: the machine name, the display number, and the screen number. Typical examples are as follows:

```
:0.0
```

```
adzel:1.0
```

```
term21.solar-spice.co.uk:0.0
```

Note that the hostname (before the colon) can be blank—this is equivalent to specifying localhost. The display number represents an individual X server program. When running only a single X server, the display number is usually 0, but it is occasionally helpful to start an extra server, which will have a higher number. Finally, some X server implementations support more than one screen per display and, if so, this is specified after the period. But this option will not affect most Debian users.

The first screen managed by the first X server running on the local machine will be display :0.0, and this is the default. To specify an alternative display, the normal approach is to set the DISPLAY environment variable:

```
export DISPLAY=adzel:0.0
xclock &
```

As you might expect, this variable is automatically set to an appropriate value (:0.0) when you start an X session. It is also usually possible to specify a display for an individual application. When this is allowed, the -display switch is normally used, for example

```
xclock -display adzel:0.0 &
```

Either of these methods allows you to force an application to attempt a connection to a specific X server. However, this doesn't mean that the X server has to accept the connection: Remember that, in general, you aren't going to want other people running applications that open windows on your display. In fact, the situation is rather worse than that; once an X client is connected to a server, it can perform all kinds of operations, including grabbing shots of the screen.

There are several mechanisms by which X security can be controlled. The simplest approach is to allow or deny connections to your X server according to the computer from which they originate. This is controlled using the xhost command. The most common use of this command is to enable access to one specific computer:

```
xhost +adzel
```

It is also possible to turn off access control completely and leave your X display totally unsecured:

```
xhost +
```

But bear in mind that when you grant permission to connect to an X display, you are opening a *big* security hole. In particular, you should consider disabling access control only when your machine is connected to a private network. Remember that UNIX computers are multiuser, so when you allow connections from a specific machine, you are granting access to all the users with accounts on that machine.

In practice, modern X security is achieved using a system of *magic cookies*, which are randomly generated strings provided by X servers when they first start up. Possessing the appropriate cookie gives you permission to connect to the X server that generated it. Magic cookies are stored in the file .Xauthority in your home directory. This file is normally manipulated using the xauth command. For instance, you can view the current entries using this command:

```
xauth list
```

When you start a normal X session under Debian (using either `startx` or a display manager program), a magic cookie is automatically generated and added to your `.Xauthority` file. If you log on to another machine, you can grant it permission to access your X display by transferring the cookie to that machine.

If you don't want to worry about cookies, there is an easier and even safer way of granting access to other computers—using the ssh program. If you are using an X session, run the `ssh` command in order to log on to another computer. It will automatically set up a special connection-forwarding service, meaning that X applications that you run on the remote machine automatically appear on the appropriate display.

One case in which many users—even those who don't have a network—might want to investigate X authentication is when running a shell as a different user from the one who started the X session, but still on the same machine. It is easy to quickly run a shell as an alternative user using the su command. Suppose, for instance, that you want to quickly alter a system-wide configuration file. You type

```
xterm -e su &
```

The su command, used here without any parameters, prompts for the root password and, if correct, starts a root shell. If you just want to run a text-console program (the vi editor, for instance), there's no problem. But suppose your favorite editor is an X client program. Since there will not be a correct `.Xauthority` file in the root account's home directory, your connection to the X server will be refused unless you have specifically allowed connections from *any* user on the local machine, using the xhost command. Fortunately, the root account's privileged status (it can read any file owned by any user on the system) provides a solution in this case. You can tell X clients to look for the `.Xauthority` file in a location other than the default using a command such as

```
export XAUTHORITY=/home/thomas/.Xauthority
```

Note, however, that this solution works only for the root account. If you want to run an X client using some other account, you will either have to deal with magic cookies yourself or start a new X session. In general, the latter option may be easiest.

Extra X

How do you run more than a single X display? If you want to start a new X session as a different user, the simplest method is to switch back to a text console by pressing Control+Alt+F1. (This is basically the same mechanism as when switching from one text console to another, but since the Alt+function key combinations can be used by some X applications, Control+Alt is used instead.) You can now log on as another user, and then you can start an X session using a command such as

```
startx — :1
```

This is the same as the normal command for starting a standalone X session, except that extra options are specified to tell the startx program to run an X server on display number 1, rather than the default 0. If you are running more than one X server at the same time, you can switch between them in much the same way that you switch between text consoles. The first X server you start will normally run on console 7 (Control+Alt+F7 will take you there), the second will be on console 8, and so on.

An extra X server can occasionally be useful when you encounter an X application that requires a specific color depth of the screen. The XFree86 system doesn't allow you to change the color depth of a running server. You normally use the value specified by the DefaultColorDepth option in your /etc/X11/XF86Config file (see Chapter 6), which defaults to eight bits per pixel (256 colors) if you don't specify a value. Suppose that you normally use a 16-bit per pixel display, but you suddenly find an application that requires a different color depth (there are a few programs, particularly games, that are fussy about such things). You can leave your normal X server running and start another one using this command:

```
startx — :1 -bpp 8
```

Note that running an extra X server *isn't* the right solution if you just want some extra space to work with windowed applications. Most modern window managers offer some form of workspace facility. These are separate desktops, each of which can have its own set of windows. You can switch between workspaces at any time using a simple keypress or mouse click. WindowMaker offers a powerful workspace-management system, accessible from the Workspaces section of the root menu.

Remote Display Management

If you have more than one computer on your network, and one of them (in this example named adzel) is running an X display manager, try typing the following at another computer on the network:

```
X :0 -query adzel
```

The X is actually the X server itself. You can specify any currently unused display number, if you are already running an X server on display 0. The -query option causes the X server to use a special protocol to communicate with a display manager running on the specified machine. Once the server has started, you should see the X display manager screen for the machine named adzel.

If you enter a username and password, you will start an X session where the server is running on your local computer, but all the client programs (including the window manager) are running on the remote machine. The local computer has become an *X terminal*. This approach allows several users to share a single powerful machine, while still running the full range of X applications. In the past, the solution of installing a few powerful UNIX servers plus dedicated X terminals for each user was popular for large commercial and academic sites. Today, the falling cost of powerful PCs and workstations has made client-server solutions a little less popular. But if you have an old PC with a good graphics card and monitor, it might well be a good candidate for an X terminal on your home network.

For more information on exactly how the relationship between the X terminal machine and the display manager works, read the manual page for the standard X display manager (xdm). Perhaps the most important configuration options are found in the file /etc/X11/xdm/Xaccess. The display manager checks this file before accepting any request to manage a remote display. By default, the Debian Xaccess file includes a line that contains just a * character, indicating that any machine can act as an X terminal. Obviously, a remote user will still need to enter his name and password before using the machine. But for extra security, you can delete the * and replace it with a list of specific machines that are allowed to connect.

Customizing Your Menus

Most graphical user interfaces provide some mechanism for launching applications. A common concept, provided by many X11 window managers, is the *root menu*, which is accessed by right-clicking the desktop background (see Figure 10.1). This can be considered equivalent to the Start menu of Windows systems. This section covers the GNU WindowMaker system, but many other window managers and application-launching panels offer menus that can be customized in similar ways.

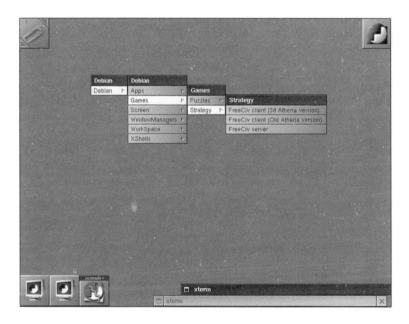

Figure 10.1

The default WindowMaker root menu on a newly installed Debian system. The menu is automatically updated when you add new packages.

WindowMaker menu definitions, together with other systemwide default files for the program, are stored in the directory /etc/X11/WindowMaker. The basic root menu itself is defined by the file menu.hook. You can take a look at this file for an example of a complex WindowMaker menu definition. But this file is automatically re-created every time a new package is installed, so if you try to edit it yourself, your changes will soon get lost.

More usefully, the `menu.hook` file contains directives that force the reading of two other files, `menu.prehook` and `menu.posthook`. These are *not* automatically generated. As the names suggest, entries added to `menu.prehook` appear before the automatically generated section, while `menu.posthook` entries come afterward. As a simple example, try adding a section to one of these files, like this:

```
Dialup MENU
  "Connect (Default)" EXEC pon
  "Connect (MyISP)" EXEC pon myisp
  "Disconnect" EXEC poff
Dialup END
```

Having edited a menu definition file, you will want to select the Restart option from the WindowManagers section of the root menu. This example section offers a simple interface for controlling dial-up Internet connections, as shown in Figure 10.2.

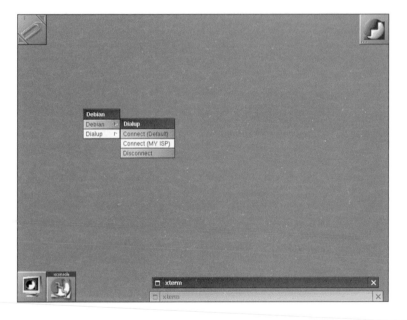

Figure 10.2

Adding a few lines to menu.posthook allows easy control of dial-up connections.

In the previous example, the WindowMaker EXEC command is used to run the programs you want. This is fine for programs like pon, which normally don't produce any output, and also for X Window System applications that open their own windows. But for programs designed to run on a text console, simply running them in this way will lose any output they produce. For instance, you might want to add an option to your Dialup menu that runs fetchmail. This program produces progress messages as your mail is retrieved. You can watch the process by starting the program in an xterm window. For instance

```
"Fetch mail" EXEC xterm -T "Fetching mail..." -e fetchmail -a
```

The -T option of the xterm program sets the title of the window, while the -e option specifies a command to execute once the window is open.

So far, the chapter has concentrated on editing system-wide default menus. You must be logged on using the root account in order to edit these files, and they affect all WindowMaker users on the system. You might want to give each user a menu for personal use. A typical way to do this is to add the following line to menu.posthook:

```
"Personal" OPEN_MENU ~/.windowmaker.menu
```

Note that ~ is UNIX shorthand for the current user's home directory. OPEN_MENU is a WindowMaker command just like EXEC in the previous example, but it allows you to direct the system to a submenu defined in a separate file. Individual users can now create a .windowmaker.menu file that might look like this:

```
Thomas MENU
    "Server" EXEC xterm -T "My server" -e telnet server.my.net
    "Info book" EXEC ghostview ~/info-theory/book.ps
Thomas END
```

This command now gives you a root menu such as the one shown in Figure 10.3.

You might be wondering where the menu.hook file comes from, and how it gets rebuilt. If so, take a look at menu, a Debian-specific program that interacts with the main packaging system. Whenever you install a Debian package that includes a program that should be added to the root menu, it adds a small file (menufile) to the directory /usr/lib/menu. The package installation script then runs the update-menus command. This command reads all the menufiles and then automatically generates not only the WindowMaker menu.hook file, but equivalent files for any other window managers and application launchers you have installed. As an alternative to manually editing configuration files for individual programs, you can create your own menufiles—the format is documented in the /usr/doc/menu directory.

User Interface Toolkits

Graphical user interfaces are built out of common objects, sometimes called *widgets*. These might include check boxes, buttons, and scrollbars. In the X Window System, it is the client's responsibility to draw all its widgets; the server itself provides only simple drawing operations. A few programs take this responsibility quite literally and draw all their own widgets, but the vast majority of major applications use some kind of toolkit that provides a range of common widgets.

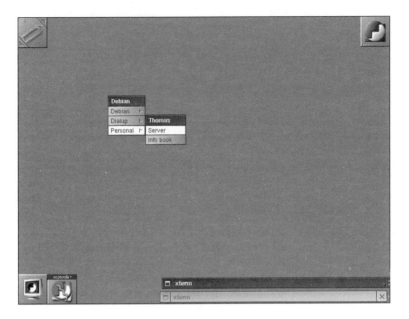

Figure 10.3

You can combine system-wide and personal menu options.

The differences between the toolkits are most important to programmers—they have different interfaces for the creation and manipulation of widgets. But there are also differences that are apparent to the normal user; different sets of widgets can look different and sometimes behave in different ways. The most important toolkits are listed here, although there are a few others that turn up from time to time:

- **Xt** (X toolkit) and **Xaw** (Athena widgetset). This combination represents the original user interface toolkit for X. It has a spartan appearance that bears little resemblance to modern user interfaces. There are several alternative implementations, for instance Xaw3D, which adds a slightly more modern 3D appearance to buttons. This toolkit is no longer used for many major applications; perhaps the best-known application that uses it is the xfig drawing package.
- **Motif**. This toolkit was popular for a long time. However, it is a commercial product, which has restricted its use on Linux-based systems. There is now a free implementation, lesstif, which is included with Debian. Even if you don't use any true Motif applications, you will still see its influence; most other user interface toolkits draw some inspiration from Motif. The following two toolkits default to drawing widgets in a style resembling Motif.
- **GTK**. This toolkit was originally written for use by the gimp graphics package but has since been adopted by the GNOME desktop environment. It is increasingly popular with developers of all kinds of application.
- **Qt.** Another toolkit that was written to allow the creation of portable applications that can be built on both UNIX and Windows platforms. Important mainly because it is used in the KDE desktop environment.

Themes

There is an increasing trend towards highly configurable graphical user interfaces. The term *theme* has been used to describe any kind of bundle of configuration data that provides a particular look and feel to your desktop. A few years back, this configuration was quite limited—you were lucky if you got to change the color scheme—but today, some programs can be reconfigured out of all recognition. To completely change the appearance of an X display, you need to reconfigure both the window manager and the client applications.

Users of the X Window System have always had a choice of window managers, and this provides one way of altering the appearance of the display. In addition, most modern window managers are *themable* to a greater or lesser extent. WindowMaker offers a typical example: The Appearance section of the root menu offers a wide selection of color schemes for the background (root window) and normal window borders. The WindowMaker drawing system allows a variety of color gradient styles, which can give some quite attractive effects. But the configurability of WindowMaker is nothing compared to that offered by the Enlightenment window manager (see Figure 10.4). This window manager aims to make just about everything configurable and, if you are suitably inclined, you can design themes ranging from the standard window manager to a science-fiction monstrosity.

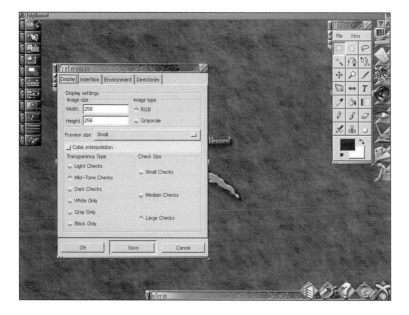

Figure 10.4

Enlightenment represents the ultimate in user interface configuration.

Configuring the appearance of X clients is a slightly more complex issue. Old applications—especially those that used the Xt or Motif toolkit—could sometimes be configured a little using the X resources mechanism. Look in the directory /usr/X11R6/lib/X11/app-defaults for some examples. But this mechanism normally just allowed simple changes of color scheme.

More recently, developers have become interested in adding theme support to the user interface toolkits. The latest versions of both Qt and GTK provide support for extensively reconfiguring the appearance of user interface widgets (see Figure 10.5).

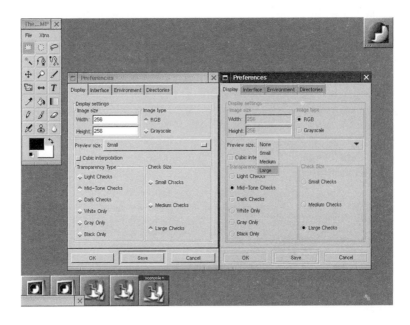

Figure 10.5

GTK (version 1.2 or later) offers configurable widget styles.

Toolkit themes can certainly make your desktop look more interesting, but if you regularly use applications written with different toolkits, you might find that installing themes gives a rather muddled appearance. In an ideal world, all toolkits might use a single mechanism for configuring the appearance of widgets but, as things stand, it is the user's responsibility to avoid clashing themes for different applications.

If you are interested in configuring the appearance of the X Window System, there is a single site that provides galleries of themes for all the major themable window managers and toolkits at http://www.themes.org/.

The Future

The X Window System has a long history. It has probably stood the test of time better than any other windowing system in common use. This is often forgotten by X users today; for instance, people complain that the old Motif user interface widgets are ugly, without stopping to remember that when they were originally designed, they had to be usable on the monochrome displays that were still common. There are some projects that aim to replace X as the primary user interface system for UNIX computers. An open source project that has attracted considerable interest can be found at http://www.berlin-consortium.org/.

However, writing off X is probably premature—it still works well today, and many developers think that it provides a very strong platform for future developments. The increasing popularity of toolkits such as GTK makes X interfaces easier to program and increasingly offers the end user choices in the look and feel of applications.

One of the weaker aspects of traditional X servers has been their font support—X has traditionally used simple bitmap fonts. With what-you-see-is-what-you-get–style productivity applications becoming more common on UNIX platforms, high-quality scaleable (that is, viewable at any size) fonts are becoming more important than ever. But it is already possible to plug in improved font support: The xfstt package offers support for the popular TrueType fonts. The forthcoming XFree86 4.0 release should offer better built-in font support.

The underlying technology of graphics displays is also changing. Many PC users now have graphics cards that provide sophisticated mechanisms for rendering 3D graphics. Making efficient use of this feature is important both to games programmers and to more serious scientific and technical applications. The standard system for programming 3D applications is the OpenGL graphics language. Better support for OpenGL programming is another issue that should be resolved in the new X server release. For more information on the development of the X server, try this site at http://www.xfree86.org/

Summary

This chapter investigated some of the power of the X Window System. Although the core X technologies are now quite old, the network-awareness and strong emphasis on flexibility mean that this window system still remains extremely powerful.

This chapter concludes the coverage of Debian configuration. The next chapter gives more information about the community of users and developers that surrounds the Debian system and includes links to useful Internet resources.

CHAPTER 11

And Finally—Welcome to the Community

If you have worked through the previous 10 chapters of this book, you now should know how to install a basic Debian GNU/Linux system and to configure many of the most important subsystems. In this chapter, you look in a little more detail at the organizations of developers working on the distribution. There are also links to a number of Internet resources that will help you to get the most out of GNU/Linux operating systems.

Remember that (with the exception of the installation and package-management systems) only a few of the Debian packages are really specific to Debian, or even to Linux systems. Indeed, many of the key programs were originally developed by users of other UNIX systems—in some cases, long before the Linux kernel was available. So, most packages have several people who are responsible for them. The original developers of a piece of software are called the *upstream maintainers*.

If the program is still under active development, the upstream maintainer is normally responsible for deciding what new features to include, and for fixing bugs. But unless the upstream maintainer happens to be a Debian user, there will probably be someone else responsible for carrying out any modifications to the Debian version of the program, and for building the Debian package files. This whole process is sometimes called *Debianization*. When reporting bugs, the Debian maintainer should be your first point of contact. The name and address of the Debian maintainer is stored within the package file. You can check the maintainer, plus many other details of any installed package, using a command such as

```
dpkg -s <packagename>
```

To a large extent, it is the group of Debian maintainers (several hundred of them) who together determine what is included in the distribution. Coordination occurs primarily by discussion on various Internet mailing lists, backed up by public voting when this is considered necessary. There is also a document called the *policy manual* that has some guidelines for maintainers. This document itself was written in a fairly open way, and is revised from time to time.

Debian Resources

The most important Debian-specific resource on the Internet is, of course, the Debian project home page at `http://www.debian.org/`.

This page contains links to information about the project, plus a list of the most important news-flashes, including information about new releases and major security alerts. If you want a little more information, a good place to start is the Debian Weekly News report at `http://www.debian.org/News/weekly/`.

This page has a regular summary of some of the most important stories from the various Debian discussion email lists. The weekly news archive is the place to look if you want some hints about the timing of the next release, or need a list of packages that recently have been added to the unstable distribution.

But if you really want to know what's going on in the Debian community, or if you want to ask questions yourself, you need to consult the mailing lists. There are a wide range of mailing lists, from the very general (`debian-user`) to the specific (`debian-laptops`, for instance). There are a few lists to which subscription is restricted only to active Debian developers, but most are open to public subscription.

There is a complete summary of available mailing lists, plus an interface for subscribing to them, linked from the Debian home page. If you are unsure whether you want to subscribe, or if you want to check out previous discussions on some topic, note that messages sent to most of the lists are automatically archived, so you can browse through them on the Web. If you have a specific question about your Debian system, it may be appropriate to post it to one of the mailing lists. But if you have just subscribed to a list, you should either wait and read (*lurk*) for a few days to get a feel for the kind of messages that are posted, or read back through the archives.

The GNU/Linux Community on the Internet

The rise of Linux-based operating systems has often been linked to the widespread availability of Internet connections. So it isn't surprising that there are many Web sites and other Internet resources that, to a greater or lesser extent, serve the GNU/Linux community. There are some obvious Linux sites; for instance at `http://www.linux.com/`.

This page links to a number of other major sites that might be of interest to GNU/Linux users. Since Linux users form a fairly cooperative community, there tends to be a high level of linking between related sites, which can be very helpful to the casual browser. In addition to global Linux sites, some pages serve more local groups of users. Notable examples include `http://www.linux.org.uk/` and `http://www.linux.de/`.

In some areas, there are local Linux User Groups (LUGs)—a Web search might reveal the existence of one in your area.

There are other sites that are more loosely connected to Linux. Perhaps the most famous example is *Slashdot* (see Figure 11.1), a popular computing and technology news site that often carries information and discussion of interest to Debian users at `http://slashdot.org/`.

One of the interesting features of this site is the "Ask Slashdot" section. While this probably isn't the right place to ask about specific installation difficulties, it is a good forum for more general Linux and UNIX issues.

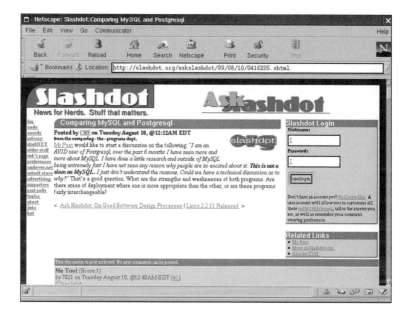

Figure 11.1

Slashdot is a popular news and discussion forum with a Linux bias.

If you are on the lookout for a specific piece of software, or you want to find details of the upstream project that leads to your favorite Debian package, *Freshmeat* (see Figure 11.2) is the place to look at `http://freshmeat.net/`.

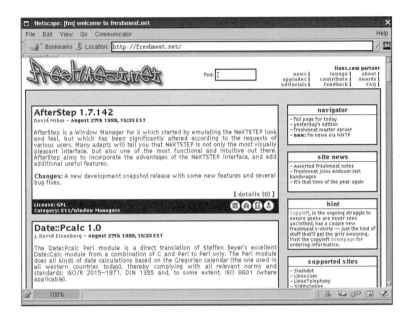

Figure 11.2

Freshmeat is a comprehensive Linux software news site.

For the more technically minded, there are also resources concerning the development of many of the key components of the GNU/Linux system. For instance, development of the Linux kernel itself is coordinated via a (very busy) mailing list, not surprisingly called `linux-kernel`. This list is mainly for the benefit of people actively developing the kernel, or testing cutting-edge development versions. But there are some efforts to summarize the major discussions on the list. If you are interested in the kernel, take a look at `http://kt.linuxcare.com/`.

Many of the GNU project tools also have their own Web sites and mailing lists. If you are interested in any of these, look for links on the following Web site at `http://www.gnu.org/`.

This site also contains some interesting opinions on the development of the free software community, so it is worth a look even if you aren't interested in the development of specific packages.

Finally, remember that there is a huge number of lesser-known Web sites that might hold the answer to your Debian or general Linux queries, so it's worth trying a Web search. At least one search engine operator now offers a special sub-database that indexes Linux-relevant sites, `http://www.google.com/linux`.

Reporting a Bug

Debian has a good reputation as a stable, reliable distribution. In part, this reputation can be attributed to the sophisticated bug-tracking software. This software records all bug reports, and tracks their status until a package maintainer declares that they are fixed. The bug database has a home on the Web: Just browse this page, `http://www.debian.org/Bugs`.

Once you are there, you can type the name of any Debian package into a text field and obtain a complete listing of any outstanding bug reports relating to that package.

It is also possible to retrieve information on bugs by email, but this is usually more useful to package maintainers. Documentation on advanced uses of the bug tracking software is available from the home page.

If you find a bug yourself, obviously you should report it. There is a certain skill involved in writing good bug reports—the description of the problem should generally be fairly concise, but in all cases should contain enough information to help the package maintainer (or someone else) reproduce the problem. The first stage is to carry out a little experimentation yourself. Can you make the bug recur? What is the simplest sequence of commands (or input file) that triggers the problem?

Bug reports are submitted to the database as email messages. You can do this manually by following the documentation for the bug-tracking system, but it is normally easier to install the `bug` package. This package helps you to assemble a bug report in the appropriate format, and then sends it on its way. To use `bug`, you need to have an email transport system set up properly. The bug report message will have its From: line based on your computer's mail name, which you set when you installed the `exim` package. If you are not confident that this will be a valid email address, set the `EMAIL` environment variable, as described in Chapter 8, "Advanced Configuration." For instance

```
export EMAIL=nick@solar-spice.com
```

The `bug` program will also start a text editor so you can enter a description of the bug. You might want to set the `EDITOR` variable to the name of your favorite text editor.

When you run `bug`, it first will ask you for the name of the Debian package that contains the bug. It will consult the package database to determine the version of the package you are using, and also details about all those packages on which the buggy package depends. You then will be asked for a *brief* description of the bug. This will make up the Subject: line of the email message, and will appear on the bug listing Web page.

Finally, the program will start a text editor and allow you to enter all the remaining information of the bug report. At the top of the message, you will see some details of the package involved. At the bottom is an automatically generated report of your system setup. In between is a space for you to type your own report of the problem. When in doubt, it's better to give too much detail rather than too little. In the case of command-line programs, you might want to paste in a complete transcript of a typical session, showing everything you typed, and any error messages produced by the program.

Remember that if you are running the X Window System, you can paste text from an xterm into another window by selecting it, and then clicking the middle button of a three-button mouse in the place where you want the text inserted.

When you have finished, save the edited bug report and quit the editor. The bug program will then send the report. After the report reaches the bug-tracking system, it will be filed away and you will receive a reply containing the number of the bug. This number is then used to track the bug through the system. You can check the status of your bug at any time by entering its number on the bug home page.

In some cases, bugs occur as the result of giving programs some specific input file. If this is a *short* text file, there is no reason why you can't simply paste it into the text of the bug report, accompanied by a suitable explanation. For larger files, other methods are needed. If you have some personal Web pages, a good solution might be to place the problem file on your Web server, and then include the address from which the file can be downloaded as part of the report.

As a simple (and not at all serious) example of a message that could be sent to the bug tracking system, consider the following:

```
Subject: primes: reporting 4 as a prime number
Package: primes
Version: 3.14

The `primes' program is reporting 4 as a prime number whenever the
maximum value specified on the command line is divisible by 5. A
transcript follows:

  adzel:~/test$ primes -max 12
  1 2 3 5 7 11
  adzel:~/test$ primes -max 15
  1 2 3 4 5 7 11 13

— System Information
Debian Release: 2.3
Kernel Version: Linux adzel 2.2.11 #1 Tue Aug 10 18:54:05 1999 i686

Version of the packages primes depends on:
    libmagic          2.71-8      Magic math library
```

This example should give you an idea of the kind of information that's useful when you are writing a bug report by hand. If you are using the bug program, the first few lines plus the "System Information" section are generated for you, but you still need to think carefully about the content of the report.

Making a Contribution

The most obvious way to contribute either to the Debian project or to the GNU/Linux community as a whole is by programming. This doesn't necessarily need to be a very large project. If you use a piece of free software that isn't currently available as a Debian package, why not consider *Debianizing* it fully? There are several packages that contain documentation relevant to packagers:

- developers-guide
- packaging-manual
- debian-policy

If you are thinking about producing packages, you should take a look at these, and then join the debian-devel mailing list.

You can also contribute as a programmer by fixing bugs or adding features to important programs. And if you write any software of your own, consider releasing it freely under a license matching the Debian Free Software guidelines (discussed in Chapter 1, "Introducing Debian"). Incidentally, please try to avoid writing your own software license—there are already several well-known licenses to choose from, and creating another is just likely to cause confusion.

But you don't need to have programming experience to make your mark. Most Free Software projects, especially the larger ones, are always ready to welcome any volunteers. Non-programmers can manage Web sites, write documentation, or simply test new releases and answer new users' questions on the mailing lists.

And Finally...

Having installed Debian, you have access to an extremely powerful operating system with a wide range of application software. It is the end result of almost 30 years of continuous development of UNIX-like systems. Moreover, the fact that systems like Debian can be built entirely using free software is leading to serious changes in the way people think about the computer industry.

If you enjoy the power and flexibility of Debian, you might feel inspired to contribute to either Debian itself or some other free software project. You might also want to help spread the word: unlike commercial operating systems, Debian doesn't have an advertising budget. But since it is freely distributable, there is nothing to stop you from passing it on to friends.

But whatever you do with Debian, good luck, and enjoy your explorations.

APPENDIX A

Kernel Management

Although we talk about it often, the Linux kernel usually keeps a fairly low profile. The kernel is designed to run for months on end without requiring any attention, and for normal uses, most users can ignore it entirely. But sometimes it is useful to upgrade the kernel. New versions often contain fixes for bugs or security problems, and may also offer performance improvements and drivers for the latest hardware devices.

Before upgrading to the latest kernel release, however, be sure you know what you are getting. Only the *stable* kernel series (with even minor version numbers—for instance, 2.2.11) are intended for general use. Development kernels (for instance, 2.3.15) can be unreliable, and you should normally wait for the next stable series (2.4.x).

Installing a Kernel Package

As a Debian user, normally you can install a ready-compiled kernel supplied as a normal Debian package (with a name beginning with kernel-image). Because of the special role of the kernel, the latest version isn't automatically installed by dselect in the same way that other packages are upgraded. But it is easy to manually select the kernel-image package you want. At the same time, you might want to upgrade a few other packages: if you are a programmer, you should install the kernel-headers package that matches your kernel-image. Laptop owners who rely on PC Card devices should ensure that the pcmcia-modules package matches the kernel, too.

When you install a kernel-image package, the kernel itself will be installed in the /boot directory with a name like vmlinuz-2.2.11. (The z means that this is a compressed kernel file—some non-Intel platforms do not support this kernel format.)

Unlike other Debian packages, the process of installing a new kernel does *not* delete your old one, so downgrading is easy if there is a problem. For convenience, the kernel-image package installation scripts maintain some symbolic links: /vmlinuz is linked to the latest kernel file you installed, and /vmlinuz.old points to the previous version.

There are also some extra files packaged with the kernel-image. These include *loadable kernel modules*, which are extra pieces of kernel code that can be dynamically loaded into the running kernel. Most of these code pieces are drivers for peripheral hardware devices. The modules are installed in their own directory structure. Each kernel version has its own set of modules, for instance /lib/modules/2.2.11.

It is also possible to add extra modules not packaged with the main kernel. PC card drivers are the best known example, but some other drivers (especially those for sound cards) are supplied in this form, too.

After the kernel is unpacked, the installation script gives you the opportunity to generate a new /etc/lilo.conf file and reinstall the Linux loader. If Debian is the only operating system on your machine, this is usually a sensible option. But, if you have other operating systems, the generated LILO configuration file will not allow you to boot them.

The situation after installing a new kernel is basically the same as after the first time you installed Debian. One option is to accept the automatically generated configuration file, and then add extra sections to boot your additional operating systems, as described in Chapter 4, "A Basic Installation." The alternative is to answer no when asked whether you want a new boot system installed, and then to manually alter /etc/lilo.conf to boot the new kernel. You might also want to add an extra section to the file that gives you the option to boot your old kernel file. For instance, if the old kernel was version 2.2.7, you could add this section:

```
image=/boot/vmlinuz-2.2.7
        label=old
        read-only
```

This means that if the new kernel causes any trouble, you can boot the system using the old kernel just by typing **old** at the LILO boot: prompt.

Whichever option you choose, remember that after manually editing /etc/lilo.conf, you need to type the following:

```
lilo
```

This command reads the configuration file and reinstalls the Linux loader. If you don't do this, your changes are ignored. The exception to this rule is if you are simply accepting the automatically generated configuration, in which case the kernel-image installation script automatically runs lilo. Once you are happy with the configuration, you can use the shutdown command to reboot the machine, and then test the new kernel. If you want to double-check which kernel version is in use, type the following:

```
uname -a
```

Doing It Yourself

A few years ago, virtually all Linux users compiled their own kernels from source code. Various developments—especially the movement of peripheral hardware drivers from the kernel into separate loadable modules—mean that today, the majority of users can make do with precompiled kernels. But building your own kernel can still be useful if you have some obscure hardware device that's not supported by the standard configuration.

There can also be performance gains. By building your own kernel, you can exclude unnecessary drivers and ensure that the kernel is optimized for the processor family you are using. Especially on Intel systems, the precompiled kernels represent the lowest common denominator, which will work on anything from a 386 upwards, but which might not run as fast as a kernel specifically optimized to take advantage of the latest Pentium IIs. Finally, you might need to recompile your kernel if you want to take advantage of a multi-processor PC. Standard kernels often only make use of one processor. You can check whether multi-processor support is enabled by typing the following:

```
uname -a
```

Check to see whether the kernel version includes the letters SMP (symmetric multi-processing). SMP kernels run fine on computers with only one processor, but there may be a slight speed penalty due to the extra *locking* code needed to prevent multiple processors from interfering with one another.

There are two slightly different approaches you can take to building a new kernel. The traditional approach uses just the standard Linux development tools and leaves you with a kernel file, which you must install manually. Debian offers an alternative approach: a package called kernel-package provides a set of scripts that allow you to build your own kernel-image packages. You can then install these packages just like kernel images from the official Debian archives. If you want to ignore the Debian-specific scripts, just install the latest kernel source and then read the Kernel-HOWTO document. Otherwise, read on.

Kernel Prerequisites

Before you start, you need to have all the normal Linux development tools installed—notably the C compiler (gcc) and make. You also want the following:

- kernel-package (not usually found on Debian CD-ROMs—download it from the archive instead)
- bin86 used in part of the kernel build process

- `fakeroot` command
- `tcl` and `tk`—for the graphical kernel configuration interface

Selected kernel releases are available from the Debian archives in packages with names beginning with `kernel-source`. Note that these are found alongside normal binary packages, not in the source sections of the archives. If you install one of these packages, it installs the kernel source as a `.tar.gz` file in the `/usr/src` directory. Alternatively, you can download the kernel source from the official site:

```
http://www.kernel.org/
```

The kernel.org sites are extensively mirrored, so use a nearby site if you can. You then need to unpack the kernel source. For example

```
tar zxf /usr/src/kernel-source-2.2.11.tar.gz
```

It is traditional to place the Linux source code in the directory `/usr/src/linux`, but if you are using `kernel-package` you probably *shouldn't* do this. You don't need to be logged on as root to compile a kernel, and there is no reason not to place the source in your home directory.

Configuring the Kernel

If your kernel source was supplied as a Debian package, it will unpack in a directory called `kernel-source-<version>`. Kernel source from other sites is normally left in a directory called `linux`. In either case, change into the directory and type the following:

```
make xconfig
```

There will be a short delay, and then the windowed kernel configuration interface will start (see Figure A.1).

If you don't want an X Window System interface, you can also try

```
make menuconfig
```

which provides a console interface similar to the Debian installer. If you think even that is excessive, you can still use the old text-only configuration system by typing the following:

```
make config
```

In any case, you should work systematically through the options. There is a huge number of options, but a large portion of them are just drivers for specific hardware devices—you should know straight away whether these apply to your computer. When in doubt, try the online help: most of the important kernel options are well documented there. Some of the most vital options are also covered in the Kernel-HOWTO document.

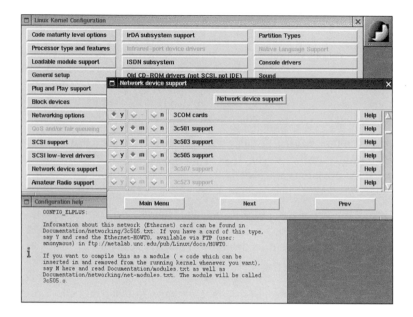

Figure A.1

The xconfig kernel configuration interface.

For many of the kernel options (especially device drivers), you are given three options: yes, no, or module. Answering yes builds that component as a standard part of the kernel. On the other hand, answering module (m) compiles a loadable kernel module, which will be automatically added to the running kernel when it is needed. Modular kernels can save a little memory if rarely used drivers are only loaded when they are needed, and are a good idea if you want to build a single kernel for use on several machines with different hardware configurations.

Some users prefer the simplicity of a *monolithic* (no modules) kernel. If you modularize your kernel, bear in mind that those modules need to be loaded from disk once the kernel is running. So modularizing the hard disk controller drivers or the ext2 filesystem is likely to be a bad idea. On the other hand, modular network drivers are normally safe. When you have finished, click on the Save and exit option. Finally, type the following:

```
/usr/sbin/make-kpkg clean
```

This command cleans up any temporary files in the kernel source directories. You now are ready to compile your first kernel.

Making a Kernel Package

If you are using the kernel-package system, you can build the kernel (plus any modules) with a single command. For instance:

```
fakeroot /usr/sbin/make-kpkg —revision=mysystem.1.0 kernel_image
```

Note the use of the `fakeroot` command. It isn't actually part of the `kernel-package` system, but it is a general mechanism that allows some programs (including parts of the `make-kpkg` system) that normally rely on running with root privileges to work when used by normal users. By avoiding the use of the root account you ensure that no important system files would be damaged if the program ran amok. In reality, `kernel-package` probably can be considered reasonably trustworthy, but even so, it is good practice to avoid logging on as root when there is a viable alternative.

The `—revision` option is used to name `kernel-image` packages that you compile yourself differently from the official Debian packages built from the same kernel source. The full list of options accepted by the `make-kpkg` command is included in the files in the `/usr/doc/kernel-package` directory.

The Linux kernel is a major piece of software, and compiling it takes several minutes even on a fast PC. After the kernel itself is built, the program goes back and compiles any kernel components you have modularized. Finally, the kernel, its modules, and some Debian installation scripts are all packaged together in a `.deb` file, which is placed in the parent directory containing your kernel source directory. If you do any programming and rely on the `kernel-headers` package, you should build a package that matches the `kernel-image` you just built. For example

```
fakeroot /usr/sbin/make-kpkg —revision=mysystem.1.0 kernel_headers
```

When you have built your kernel packages, you can install them (as root; using `fakeroot` won't do in this case) using `dpkg`:

```
dpkg -i kernel-image-2.2.11_mysystem.1.0_i386.deb
```

Except for the exact configuration used, this `kernel-image` package will be just like those found in the Debian archive. You will see the same installation scripts, which offer you the chance to create a new `/etc/lilo.conf`. If this is the first kernel you have built, you probably want to add an extra entry to `/etc/lilo.conf`, which gives you access to an old (and tested) kernel, just in case there is a serious problem with the configuration you selected.

INDEX

Please Read Before Installing CD-ROM

What's on the Disc

The companion CD-ROM contains the Debian GNU/Linux operating system.

Debian Installation Instructions

Insert the companion CD-ROM in your system. Reboot the computer and Debian should auto run. Then follow the Debian install instructions.

If your system will not boot from CD, there are other options:

1. Boot a DOS system with CD drivers, then run boot.bat from the \install directory on the first CD.
2. Make boot floppies from the images on the first CD, in the directory \dists\slink\main\disks-i386\2.1.9-1999-03-03. The program rawrite2.exe in that directory will write the floppy images under DOS.
3. Next change to your correct CD-ROM drive.
4. Next extract the program rawrite2.exe to a floppy drive using cd d: \dists\slink\main\disks-i386\2.1.9-1999-03-03\rawrite2 -f resc1440.bin -d a:

NOTE

> d: is your CD-ROM Drive and a: is the 1.44MB floppy drive.

5. See\install\install.txt for more information, and \README.multicd for last-minute information about the multi-cd installation method.

GNU GENERAL PUBLIC LICENSE

Version 2, June 1991

Copyright © 1989, 1991 Free Software Foundation, Inc.

675 Mass Ave, Cambridge, MA 02139, USA

Preamble

The licenses for most software are designed to take away your freedom to share and change it. By contrast, the GNU General Public License is intended to guarantee your freedom to share and change free software—to make sure the software is free for all its users. This General Public License applies to most of the Free Software Foundation's software and to any other program whose authors commit to using it. (Some other Free Software Foundation software is covered by the GNU Library General Public License instead.) You can apply it to your programs, too.

When we speak of free software, we are referring to freedom, not price. Our General Public Licenses are designed to make sure that you have the freedom to distribute copies of free software (and charge for this service if you wish), that you receive source code or can get it if you want it, that you can change the software or use pieces of it in new free programs; and that you know you can do these things.

To protect your rights, we need to make restrictions that forbid anyone to deny you these rights or to ask you to surrender the rights. These restrictions translate to certain responsibilities for you if you distribute copies of the software, or if you modify it.

For example, if you distribute copies of such a program, whether gratis or for a fee, you must give the recipients all the rights that you have. You must make sure that they, too, receive or can get the source code. And you must show them these terms so they know their rights.

We protect your rights with two steps: (1) copyright the software, and (2) offer you this license which gives you legal permission to copy, distribute and/or modify the software.

Also, for each author's protection and ours, we want to make certain that everyone understands that there is no warranty for this free software. If the software is modified by someone else and passed on, we want its recipients to know that what they have is not the original, so that any problems introduced by others will not reflect on the original authors' reputations.

Finally, any free program is threatened constantly by software patents. We wish to avoid the danger that redistributors of a free program will individually obtain patent licenses, in effect making the program proprietary. To prevent this, we have made it clear that any patent must be licensed for everyone's free use or not licensed at all.

The precise terms and conditions for copying, distribution and modification follow.

GNU General Public License

TERMS AND CONDITIONS FOR COPYING, DISTRIBUTION AND MODIFICATION

This License applies to any program or other work which contains a notice placed by the copyright holder saying it may be distributed under the terms of this General Public License. The "Program," below, refers to any such program or work, and a "work based on the Program" means either the Program or any derivative work under copyright law: that is to say, a work containing the Program or a portion of it, either verbatim or with modifications and/or translated into another language. (Hereinafter, translation is included without limitation in the term "modification".) Each licensee is addressed as "you".

Activities other than copying, distribution and modification are not covered by this License; they are outside its scope. The act of running the Program is not restricted, and the output from the Program is covered only if its contents constitute a work based on the Program (independent of having been made by running the Program). Whether that is true depends on what the Program does.

1. You may copy and distribute verbatim copies of the Program's source code as you receive it, in any medium, provided that you conspicuously and appropriately publish on each copy an appropriate copyright notice and disclaimer of warranty; keep intact all the notices that refer to this License and to the absence of any warranty; and give any other recipients of the Program a copy of this License along with the Program.

You may charge a fee for the physical act of transferring a copy, and you may at your option offer warranty protection in exchange for a fee.

2. You may modify your copy or copies of the Program or any portion of it, thus forming a work based on the Program, and copy and distribute such modifications or work under the terms of Section 1 above, provided that you also meet all of these conditions:

    a) You must cause the modified files to carry prominent notices stating that you changed the files and the date of any change.

    b) You must cause any work that you distribute or publish, that in whole or in part contains or is derived from the Program or any part thereof, to be licensed as a whole at no charge to all third parties under the terms of this License.

    c) If the modified program normally reads commands interactively when run, you must cause it, when started running for such interactive use in the most ordinary way, to print or display an announcement including an appropriate copyright notice and a notice that there is no warranty (or else, saying that you provide a warranty) and that users may redistribute the program under these conditions, and telling the user how to view a copy of this License. (Exception: if the Program itself is interactive but does not normally print such an announcement, your work based on the Program is not required to print an announcement.)

These requirements apply to the modified work as a whole. If identifiable sections of that work are not derived from the Program, and can be reasonably considered independent and separate works in themselves, then this License, and its terms, do not apply to those sections when you distribute them as separate works. But when you distribute the same sections as part of a whole which is a work based on the Program, the distribution of the whole must be on the terms of this License, whose permissions for other licensees extend to the entire whole, and thus to each and every part regardless of who wrote it.

Thus, it is not the intent of this section to claim rights or contest your rights to work written entirely by you; rather, the intent is to exercise the right to control the distribution of derivative or collective works based on the Program.

In addition, mere aggregation of another work not based on the Program with the Program (or with a work based on the Program) on a volume of a storage or distribution medium does not bring the other work under the scope of this License.

3. You may copy and distribute the Program (or a work based on it, under Section 2) in object code or executable form under the terms of Sections 1 and 2 above provided that you also do one of the following:

   a) Accompany it with the complete corresponding machine-readable source code, which must be distributed under the terms of Sections 1 and 2 above on a medium customarily used for software interchange; or,

   b) Accompany it with a written offer, valid for at least three years, to give any third party, for a charge no more than your cost of physically performing source distribution, a complete machine-readable copy of the corresponding source code, to be distributed under the terms of Sections 1 and 2 above on a medium customarily used for software interchange; or,

   c) Accompany it with the information you received as to the offer to distribute corresponding source code. (This alternative is allowed only for non-commercial distribution and only if you received the program in object code or executable form with such an offer, in accord with Subsection b above.)

The source code for a work means the preferred form of the work for making modifications to it. For an executable work, complete source code means all the source code for all modules it contains, plus any associated interface definition files, plus the scripts used to control compilation and installation of the executable. However, as a special exception, the source code distributed need not include anything that is normally distributed (in either source or binary form) with the major components (compiler, kernel, and so on) of the operating system on which the executable runs, unless that component itself accompanies the executable.

If distribution of executable or object code is made by offering access to copy from a designated place, then offering equivalent access to copy the source code from the same place counts as distribution of the source code, even though third parties are not compelled to copy the source along with the object code.

4. You may not copy, modify, sublicense, or distribute the Program except as expressly provided under this License. Any attempt otherwise to copy, modify, sublicense or distribute the Program is void, and will automatically terminate your rights under this License. However, parties who have received copies, or rights, from you under this License will not have their licenses terminated so long as such parties remain in full compliance.

5. You are not required to accept this License, since you have not signed it. However, nothing else grants you permission to modify or distribute the Program or its derivative works. These actions are prohibited by law if you do not accept this License. Therefore, by modifying or distributing the Program (or any work based on the Program), you indicate your acceptance of this License to do so, and all its terms and conditions for copying, distributing or modifying the Program or works based on it.

6. Each time you redistribute the Program (or any work based on the Program), the recipient automatically receives a license from the original licensor to copy, distribute or modify the Program subject to these terms and conditions. You may not impose any further restrictions on the recipients' exercise of the rights granted herein. You are not responsible for enforcing compliance by third parties to this License.

7. If, as a consequence of a court judgment or allegation of patent infringement or for any other reason (not limited to patent issues), conditions are imposed on you (whether by court order, agreement or otherwise) that contradict the conditions of this License, they do not excuse you from the conditions of this License. If you cannot distribute so as to satisfy simultaneously your obligations under this License and any other pertinent obligations, then as a consequence you may not distribute the Program at all. For example, if a patent license would not permit royalty-free redistribution of the Program by all those who receive copies directly or indirectly through you, then the only way you could satisfy both it and this License would be to refrain entirely from distribution of the Program.

If any portion of this section is held invalid or unenforceable under any particular circumstance, the balance of the section is intended to apply and the section as a whole is intended to apply in other circumstances.

It is not the purpose of this section to induce you to infringe any patents or other property right claims or to contest validity of any such claims; this section has the sole purpose of protecting the integrity of the free software distribution system, which is implemented by public license practices. Many people have made generous contributions to the wide range of software distributed through that system in reliance on consistent application of that system; it is up to the author/donor to decide if he or she is willing to distribute software through any other system and a licensee cannot impose that choice.

This section is intended to make thoroughly clear what is believed to be a consequence of the rest of this License.

8. If the distribution and/or use of the Program is restricted in certain countries either by patents or by copyrighted interfaces, the original copyright holder who places the Program under this License may add an explicit geographical distribution limitation excluding those countries, so that distribution is permitted only in or among countries not thus excluded. In such case, this License incorporates the limitation as if written in the body of this License.

9. The Free Software Foundation may publish revised and/or new versions of the General Public License from time to time. Such new versions will be similar in spirit to the present version, but may differ in detail to address new problems or concerns.

Each version is given a distinguishing version number. If the Program specifies a version number of this License which applies to it and "any later version", you have the option of following the terms and conditions either of that version or of any later version published by the Free Software Foundation. If the Program does not specify a version number of this License, you may choose any version ever published by the Free Software Foundation.

10. If you wish to incorporate parts of the Program into other free programs whose distribution conditions are different, write to the author to ask for permission. For software which is copyrighted by the Free Software Foundation, write to the Free Software Foundation; we sometimes make exceptions for this. Our decision will be guided by the two goals of preserving the free status of all derivatives of our free software and of promoting the sharing and reuse of software generally.

No Warranty

11. BECAUSE THE PROGRAM IS LICENSED FREE OF CHARGE, THERE IS NO WARRANTY FOR THE PROGRAM, TO THE EXTENT PERMITTED BY APPLICABLE LAW. EXCEPT WHEN OTHERWISE STATED IN WRITING THE COPYRIGHT HOLDERS AND/OR OTHER PARTIES PROVIDE THE PROGRAM "AS IS" WITHOUT WARRANTY OF ANY KIND, EITHER EXPRESSED OR IMPLIED, INCLUDING, BUT NOT LIMITED TO, THE IMPLIED WARRANTIES OF MERCHANTABILITY AND FITNESS FOR A PARTICULAR PURPOSE. THE ENTIRE RISK AS TO THE QUALITY AND PERFORMANCE OF THE PROGRAM IS WITH YOU. SHOULD THE PROGRAM PROVE DEFECTIVE, YOU ASSUME THE COST OF ALL NECESSARY SERVICING, REPAIR OR CORRECTION.

12. IN NO EVENT UNLESS REQUIRED BY APPLICABLE LAW OR AGREED TO IN WRITING WILL ANY COPYRIGHT HOLDER, OR ANY OTHER PARTY WHO MAY MODIFY AND/OR REDISTRIBUTE THE PROGRAM AS PERMITTED ABOVE, BE LIABLE TO YOU FOR DAMAGES, INCLUDING ANY GENERAL, SPECIAL, INCIDENTAL OR CONSEQUENTIAL DAMAGES ARISING OUT OF THE USE OR INABILITY TO USE THE PROGRAM (INCLUDING BUT NOT LIMITED TO LOSS OF DATA OR DATA BEING RENDERED INACCURATE OR LOSSES SUSTAINED BY YOU OR THIRD PARTIES OR A FAILURE OF THE PROGRAM TO OPERATE WITH ANY OTHER PROGRAMS), EVEN IF SUCH HOLDER OR OTHER PARTY HAS BEEN ADVISED OF THE POSSIBILITY OF SUCH DAMAGES.

End of Terms and Conditions

Linux and the GNU System

The GNU project started 12 years ago with the goal of developing a complete free UNIX-like operating system. "Free" refers to freedom, not price; it means you are free to run, copy, distribute, study, change, and improve the software.

A UNIX-like system consists of many different programs. We found some components already available as free software—for example, X Windows and TeX. We obtained other components by helping to convince their developers to make them free—for example, the Berkeley network utilities. Other components we wrote specifically for GNU—for example, GNU Emacs, the GNU C compiler, the GNU C library, Bash, and Ghostscript. The components in this last category are "GNU software".

The GNU system consists of all three categories together.

The GNU project is not just about developing and distributing free software. The heart of the GNU project is an idea: that software should be free, and that the users' freedom is worth defending. For if people have freedom but do not value it, they will not keep it for long. In order to make freedom last, we have to teach people to value it.

The GNU project's method is that free software and the idea of users' freedom support each other. We develop GNU software, and as people encounter GNU programs or the GNU system and start to use them, they also think about the GNU idea. The software shows that the idea can work in practice. People who come to agree with the idea are likely to write additional free software. Thus, the software embodies the idea, spreads the idea, and grows from the idea.

This method was working well—until someone combined the Linux kernel with the GNU system (which still lacked a kernel), and called the combination a "Linux system."

The Linux kernel is a free UNIX-compatible kernel written by Linus Torvalds. It was not written specifically for the GNU project, but the Linux kernel and the GNU system work together well. In fact, adding Linux to the GNU system brought the system to completion: it made a free UNIX-compatible operating system available for use.

But ironically, the practice of calling it a "Linux system" undermines our method of communicating the GNU idea. At first impression, a "Linux system" sounds like something completely distinct from the "GNU system." And that is what most users think it is.

Most introductions to the "Linux system" acknowledge the role played by the GNU software components. But they don't say that the system as a whole is more or less the same GNU system that the GNU project has been compiling for a decade. They don't say that the idea of a free UNIX-like system originates from the GNU project. So most users don't know these things.

This leads many of those users to identify themselves as a separate community of "Linux users", distinct from the GNU user community.

They use all of the GNU software; in fact, they use almost all of the GNU system; but they don't think of themselves as GNU users, and they may not think about the GNU idea.

It leads to other problems as well—even hampering cooperation on software mainte-nance. Normally when users change a GNU program to make it work better on a par-ticular system, they send the change to the maintainer of that program; then they work with the maintainer, explaining the change, arguing for it and sometimes rewriting it, to get it installed.

But people who think of themselves as "Linux users" are more likely to release a forked "Linux-only" version of the GNU program, and consider the job done. We want each and every GNU program to work "out of the box" on Linux-based systems; but if the users do not help, that goal becomes much harder to achieve.

So how should the GNU project respond? What should we do now to spread the idea that freedom for computer users is important?

We should continue to talk about the freedom to share and change software—and to teach other users to value these freedoms. If we enjoy having a free operating system, it makes sense for us to think about preserving those freedoms for the long term. If we enjoy having a variety of free software, it makes sense for to think about encouraging others to write additional free software, instead of additional proprietary software.

We should not accept the splitting of the community in two. Instead we should spread the word that "Linux systems" are variant GNU systems—that users of these systems are GNU users, and that they ought to consider the GNU philosophy which brought these systems into existence.

This article is one way of doing that. Another way is to use the terms "Linux-based GNU system" (or "GNU/Linux system" or "Lignux" for short) to refer to the combi-nation of the Linux kernel and the GNU system.

Copyright © 1996 Richard Stallman. (Verbatim copying and redistribution is permitted without royalty as long as this notice is preserved.)

The Linux kernel is Copyright © 1991, 1992, 1993, 1994 Linus Torvalds (others hold copyrights on some of the drivers, file systems, and other parts of the kernel) and is licensed under the terms of the GNU General Public License.

The FreeBSD Copyright

All of the documentation and software included in the 4.4BSD and 4.4BSD-Lite Releases is copyrighted by The Regents of the University of California.

Copyright 1979, 1980, 1983, 1986, 1988, 1989, 1991, 1992, 1993, 1994 The Regents of the University of California. All rights reserved.

Redistribution and use in source and binary forms, with or without modification, are permitted provided that the following conditions are met:

1. Redistributions of source code must retain the above copyright notice, this list of conditions and the following disclaimer.
2. Redistributions in binary form must reproduce the above copyright notice, this list of conditions and the following disclaimer in the documentation and/or other materials provided with the distribution.
3. All advertising materials mentioning features or use of this software must display the following acknowledgement:

This product includes software developed by the University of California, Berkeley and its contributors.

4. Neither the name of the University nor the names of its contributors may be used to endorse or promote products derived from this software without specific prior written permission.

THIS SOFTWARE IS PROVIDED BY THE REGENTS AND CONTRIBUTORS "AS IS" AND ANY EXPRESS OR IMPLIED WARRANTIES, INCLUDING, BUT NOT LIMITED TO, THE IMPLIED WARRANTIES OF MERCHANTABILITY AND FITNESS FOR A PARTICULAR PURPOSE ARE DISCLAIMED. IN NO EVENT SHALL THE REGENTS OR CONTRIBUTORS BE LIABLE FOR ANY DIRECT, INDIRECT, INCIDENTAL, SPECIAL, EXEMPLARY, OR CONSEQUENTIAL DAMAGES (INCLUDING, BUT NOT LIMITED TO, PROCUREMENT OF SUBSTITUTE GOODS OR SERVICES; LOSS OF USE, DATA, OR PROFITS; OR BUSINESS INTERRUPTION) HOWEVER CAUSED AND ON ANY THEORY OF LIABILITY, WHETHER IN CONTRACT, STRICT LIABILITY, OR TORT (INCLUDING NEGLIGENCE OR OTHERWISE) ARISING IN ANY WAY OUT OF THE USE OF THIS SOFTWARE, EVEN IF ADVISED OF THE POSSIBILITY OF SUCH DAMAGE.

The Institute of Electrical and Electronics Engineers and the American National Standards Committee X3, on Information Processing Systems have given us permission to reprint portions of their documentation.

In the following statement, the phrase "this text" refers to portions of the system documentation.

Portions of this text are reprinted and reproduced in electronic form in the second BSD Networking Software Release, from IEEE Std 1003.1-1988, IEEE Standard Portable Operating System Interface for Computer Environments (POSIX), copyright C 1988 by the Institute of Electrical and Electronics Engineers, Inc. In the event of any discrepancy between these versions and the original IEEE Standard, the original IEEE Standard is the referee document.

In the following statement, the phrase "This material" refers to portions of the system documentation.

This material is reproduced with permission from American National Standards Committee X3, on Information Processing Systems. Computer and Business Equipment Manufacturers Association (CBEMA), 311 First St., NW, Suite 500, Washington, DC 20001-2178. The developmental work of Programming Language C was completed by the X3J11 Technical Committee.

The views and conclusions contained in the software and documentation are those of the authors and should not be interpreted as representing official policies, either expressed or implied, of the Regents of the University of California.

www@FreeBSD.ORG

Date: 1997/07/01   03:52:05